Republic of Apples, Democracy of Oranges

MĀNOA 31:1   UNIVERSITY   HONOLULU
OF HAWAI'I
PRESS

REPUBLIC OF APPLES, DEMOCRACY OF ORANGES

New Eco-poetry from China and the United States

Frank Stewart

SERIES EDITOR

Tony Barnstone
Ming Di

GUEST EDITORS

Mānoa: A Pacific Journal of International Writing

Editor Frank Stewart

Managing Editor Pat Matsueda

Associate Editor Noah Perales-Estoesta

Staff Silvana Mae Bautista, Soumya Rachel Shailendra

Designer and Art Editor Barbara Pope

Consulting Editors
Robert Bringhurst, Barry Lopez, W. S. Merwin, Carol Moldaw, Michael Nye,
Naomi Shihab Nye, Gary Snyder, Julia Steele, Arthur Sze, Michelle Yeh

Corresponding Editors for Asia and the Pacific
CAMBODIA Sharon May
CHINA Chen Zeping, Karen Gernant
HONG KONG Shirley Geok-lin Lim
INDONESIA John H. McGlynn
JAPAN Leza Lowitz
KOREA Bruce Fulton
NEW ZEALAND AND SOUTH PACIFIC Vilsoni Hereniko, Alexander Mawyer
PACIFIC LATIN AMERICA Noah Perales-Estoesta
PHILIPPINES Alfred A. Yuson
SOUTH ASIA Alok Bhalla, Sukrita Paul Kumar
WESTERN CANADA Trevor Carolan

Advisors Laura E. Lyons, Robert Shapard

Founded in 1988 by Robert Shapard and Frank Stewart

Mānoa is published twice a year and is available in print and online for both individuals
and institutions. Subscribe at https://www.uhpress.hawaii.edu/title/manoa/. Please visit
http://muse.jhu.edu/journals/manoa to browse issues and tables of contents online.

Claims for non-receipt of issues will be honored if claim is made within 180 days of the month
of publication. Thereafter, the regular back-issue rate will be charged for replacement. Inquiries
are received at uhpjourn@hawaii.edu or by phone at 1-888-UHPRESS or 808-956-8833.

Mānoa gratefully acknowledges the support of the University of Hawai‘i and the University
of Hawai‘i College of Languages, Linguistics, and Literature; with additional support from
Hawai‘i State Foundation on Culture and the Arts and Mānoa Foundation.

manoa.hawaii.edu/manoajournal
https://www.uhpress.hawaii.edu/title/manoa/
muse.jhu.edu
jstor.org

HAWAI‘I
STATE FOUNDATION on
CULTURE and the ARTS

THE MĀNOA FOUNDATION

CONTENTS

Dismantling the Temple,
Qingtan, 2001.
Photograph by Linda Butler.

This temple was dismantled, then its
timbers, bricks, and tiles were carefully
numbered, taken by barge to Maoping,
and put into storage. It was rebuilt
at a new site overlooking the Three
Gorges Dam.

TONY BARNSTONE

Han Shan's Transparent Eyeball:
The Asian Roots of American Eco-poetry

In 1984, I was twenty-three years old, the sort of man that the hermit-poet
and irascible social critic Han Shan[1] (c. 700–800 CE) would have described
in this way:

1. There is debate
about whether the
person Han Shan
ever existed and if
the poems that bear
his name are merely
a tradition of poetry
in which multiple
authors wrote.

> A graceful and handsome young man,
> well-versed in canons and histories,
> everyone calls him a teacher,
> or addresses him as a scholar,
> but he fails to get an official post,
> and doesn't know how to use a plow.
> He wears only a shabby gown in winter,
> totally ruined by books.
> (Barnstone 2005, 202)

I was ruined by books, using my college degree in literature to do data entry,
temp work, window-washing in Silicon Valley, even working in a granola
factory in Santa Cruz, California, which I know sounds like it must be a joke.

Yet the books that had ruined me also landed me my first teaching job, at
the Beijing Foreign Studies Institute, in a China that was testing out how much
it wanted to open up to Western culture and economic structures in the period
following the death of Mao Zedong.

A Tangle of Roots

Though I was barely older than my students, I found myself
teaching American and British literature, as well as English language and
conversation, and I loved it. Partway through the first term, one of my best
students in the language class, a young woman deeply interested in our con-
versations about life in America versus life in China, asked me a question that
set me back on my heels a bit: "Professor Barnstone, we have heard this word
'individualism,' but we don't know what it means. Can you tell us?"

If I had known more at the time, I would have talked about the Chinese
tradition of individualism, about the celebration of creative innovation in
Chinese ars poeticas, and about the way in which Daoism provided an outlet

for eccentrics and nonconformists who didn't fit into Confucian social and familial structures. I might have quoted the Chinese sayings "You can't build a house inside a house" or "If you follow someone, you will always be behind" (Barnstone 1996, 48). But, as I recall, I answered the question by discussing Ralph Waldo Emerson's essay "Self-Reliance."

Not long after, this student ceased coming to class. I wondered why, but didn't know until I chanced to meet her in the hallway between classes. I stopped her and cried, "What happened to you? Where did you go? You seemed to like the class so much."

"I'm sorry, I'm sorry, Tony," she whispered hurriedly. "I asked too many questions in your class. Someone has denounced me to the Party. I can't be seen talking to you."

And she rushed off, ducking her head.

It was a different China then than it is now, one where the nail that sticks up was more likely to get hammered down, where individuated clothes and hairstyles were still politically dangerous to wear, and where asking the wrong question could bring the weight of the Party down upon you. It saddened me.

Decades later, this story still saddens me. It does so because this young student suffered for evincing an interest in what a later political campaign would call "spiritual pollution" coming from the West. And yet, this tradition of individual idealism is also deeply rooted in her own Chinese culture. In fact, it emerges in the West in part because of the influence of Eastern religious and philosophical thought.

Like people, ideas travel. And they emigrate. And they take root. And they change. And some part of them remains connected to their homeland.

"But what does all of this have to do with eco-poetry?" you could ask.

I would assert that modern and contemporary American eco-poetry sprouts directly from the American Transcendentalist tradition of Walt Whitman, Henry David Thoreau, Ralph Waldo Emerson, and others.[2] These authors were deeply concerned with questions of how the poetic life is connected to the natural life; how to live with what today we would call a small carbon footprint, but which Thoreau called "economy"; and how to connect spiritually to nature despite living in a commercialized society. Yet, the Transcendentalists' ecological ideas themselves sprout from a double root: Asian as well as Western literature and philosophy.

Contemporary Chinese eco-poetry emerges from the same Asian sources—Daoist and Buddhist ideas of self and nature—but often adds a note of parody, sadness, and irony that reflects how those ideas can be lost in the contemporary urbanized, polluted, and industrial human environment.

This volume of Chinese and American eco-poetries, *Republic of Apples, Democracy of Oranges*, is an experiment to see what happens when you put into one volume two contemporary groups of eco-poets—Chinese and American—whose work is sustained by roots that are historically and intellectually intertwined. With some luck, these poets' local eco-poetic geographies might suggest a global vision.

2. Many critics have observed the same thing, in part because the Transcendentalists in their major texts make it clear that they learned at the feet of the Asian masters. The article by Lewis and Bicknell included in the list of sources, and its bibliography, are good launchpads for those interested in the subject.

The Double Mirror

We think of the Transcendentalists as quintessentially American types, in terms that Emerson, Whitman, and Thoreau themselves defined. They are individualistic, self-reliant, and free-thinking. They are willing to take peaceful, civic action so that their lives conform to their deep ethical beliefs rooted in a spiritual force in nature. It is tempting to think of these ideas as the fruit of the Reformation's focus on one's personal relationship with God and of the Enlightenment's search for ways of constructing an ethical state that respects the rights of the individual. Yet these traits are also characteristic of Asian philosophers and divines such as Buddha, Laozi, Confucius, Mencius, and the authors of the Indian Vedas and Upanishads, all of whose work the Transcendentalists read avidly and deeply. These ideas are also at the core of ecological thought.

The eco-poetic ethic of living close to nature and rejecting the world of the marketplace and power politics is a good example. The idea traces most famously to Thoreau's *Walden,* in which he tells us he went to the woods because he wanted to live deliberately, "to live deep and suck out all the marrow of life" by paring down and simplifying his life to its essentials. Certainly, Thoreau in *Walden* and Emerson in "Nature" are channeling Neoplatonism and the Romantic ideology of what Wordsworth termed "natural piety." Yet, another significant source is to be found in Asia. Thoreau kept a copy of the *Bhagavad Gita* by his bedside in the cabin and saw his experiment at Walden "as the ascetic practice of a Hindu *yogin*" (Lewis and Bicknell, 15). He writes, "The pure Walden water is mingled with the sacred water of the Ganges," and throughout *Walden* he makes clear that a central part of his inspiration to live simply and spiritually in nature comes from his desire to emulate the "ancient philosophers, Chinese, Hindoo, Persian, and Greek," who "were a class than which none has been poorer in outward riches, none so rich in inward." In particular, the Transcendentalists learned much from Asian religion and philosophy about living mindfully in the present moment, breaking the mental shackles of human thought-systems, and connecting to the greater spirit underlying the world by meditating in nature. The Transcendentalists were the original Dharma bums.

Such ecological elements within the Chinese tradition are part of the reason why, as Qingqi Wei argues, "ecocriticism encountered a place both familiar and strange" when it took root in China over the last fifteen years:

> It was perhaps the first time that a Western criticism, among dozens of others that had already traveled and settled here, had felt a sense of feeling at home, and this sensation was reported by both the Western and native ecocritics, the latter, for example, being pleased with the idea that Thoreau implies a shadow of Chuang Chou as his spiritual teacher. (538)

Cultural transmission is always a distorting mirror, whether Orientalizing or Occidentalizing. Still, it could be that the ecopoetic mirror is actually a window that opens in both directions, so that the spiritual landscape of China seeps into that of America and vice-versa.

Wei argues as much, asserting that the entry of Western eco-criticism into China was less an invasion by a foreign species than a grafting onto a native plant, and that this hybrid took root in part because the earth had already been tilled by Chinese eco-critics. Further, Chinese eco-critics found fertile ground for interpretation in the Daoist tradition of nature writing in particular: "What intrigues the Chinese interpreters involved is that traditional nature-oriented works are so 'green'—it is almost as if they had been waiting thousands of years to be reinstated via environmentalist discourse" (540).

Thus, it should not seem a strange thing that much of the poetic sensibility of Tao Qian (365–427 CE)—who is the great Daoist Chinese model for leaving the busy world and living simply in nature—could appear in *Walden*. In his poem "Return to My Country Home," Tao Qian writes that after a youth spent in "mountains and peaks," he "fell into the world's net," but once older, he returned to the essence of that childhood innocence and connection to nature: "After all those years like a beast in a cage/I've come back to the soil again" (Barnstone 2005, 76).

Later, the master Tang Dynasty poet Wang Wei (701–761 CE)—a strong influence on new Chinese and American eco-poetry—echoed Tao Qian's lines and considered him his poetic ancestor. Wang Wei writes, "In old age I ask for peace/and don't care about things of this world./I've found no good way to live/and brood about getting lost in my old forests" (Barnstone 2005, 108). And in another poem, "Bright peaks beyond the eastern forest/tell me to abandon this world" (Barnstone 2005, 108). As he writes to his friend Ji Mu:

> No need to lodge in the bright world.
> All day let your hair be tangled like reeds.
> Be lazy and in the dark about human affairs,
> in a remote place, far from the emperor.
> (Barnstone 2005, 110)

When living in nature, he quiets and calms until he becomes natural himself, not looking at nature but being in nature, part of it instead of apart from it: "Dusk comes to the silent expanse of heaven and earth/and my heart is calm like this wide river" (Barnstone 2005, 102).

Tao Qian, Wang Wei, Han Shan, and others are to the Chinese tradition what Thoreau is to the American: writers who attempted to turn their backs on "things of this world" in order to reconnect with nature and with their spiritual cores.

In contemporary poetry, we see a similar American and Chinese eco-poetic interchange. In part this is the legacy of the movement of ideas through translation. It also emerges from the movement of people in the Chinese diaspora, and from Chinese poets becoming more international, traveling more freely in the post-Mao era. In the poetry of Aku Wuwu, for example, we find poetry that is deeply rooted in the local geography and beliefs of the Yi minority Aku

Wuwu belongs to, but that also travels to America, where he remarks on the cultural appropriation of Native American customs ("Wolf Skin"), and imagines American roadkill deer as nature's revenge against human destructiveness ("Avenging Deer"). In "Wolf Skin," this revenge is associated with cultural resistance to majority Chinese culture in his Yi community.

If you look up synonyms for the word *violence,* you will find among others the words *savagery* and *wildness.* Yet, as Gary Snyder writes in *The Practice of the Wild,* "The wild—often dismissed as savage and chaotic by 'civilized' thinkers—is actually impartially, relentlessly, and beautifully formal and free. Its expression—the richness of plant and animal life on the globe, including us, the rainstorms, windstorms, and calm spring mornings—is the real world, to which we belong" (2010, x). It is with such a sense of the elided grace of the "wild" that Aku Wuwu writes his poems. He connects a pervasive cultural violence against Yi and Native American communities with the violence against nature itself. Thus, at a Native American festival he writes that he was, "Neither an enemy of the Indians, / nor their fellow folk, / yet, longed to / put on the magic Indian wolf skin." He wants to say that the Yi are like the Native Americans, yet he understands the limits of one's ability to put on another culture like a skin. In a resonant final image, he watches a white man dancing in a wolf skin, then suddenly spots in the center of the skin "a small bullet hole."

Ways of Looking at a Crow

In "Nature" Emerson bemoans the fact that we can no longer *see* nature because we have been blinded by human thought-systems. Where a poet sees a "tree," a woodcutter sees a "stick of timber." But when Emerson goes to the woods, he writes, "all mean egotism vanishes. I become a transparent eye-ball; I am nothing; I see all; the currents of the Universal Being circulate through me; I am part or particle of God." The writer in nature loses mean egotism and connects with the universal essence that runs through all life. Emerson's transparent eyeball is a great American notion, central to the spiritual ideology of our eco-poetry; yet it is also a Western localization of a commonplace of Daoist and Zen poetry.

In the Daoist poetry of Tao Qian, and in the later Zen poetry of Wang Wei and Han Shan, we see that if you sit meditating in nature long enough, then you are what your senses eat. If you sit long enough on the mountain, you become the mountain, as contemporary American poet Daniel Tobin writes, echoing famous lines by Li Bai (701–762 CE): "We sit together, the mountain and me, / until only the mountain remains." In a similar poem, Wang Wei writes that he sits "looking at moss so green / my clothes are soaked with color" (Barnstone 2005, 123, 105). It's not just that the moss is so intensely green that it seems to project its color, but also that the poet joining with nature is symbolically and spiritually stained green, and thus no longer separate from the source.

This is what the Zen poet Han Shan does when he writes a night scene about the full moon:

A swarm of stars lines up. The night is bright and deep.
Lone lamp on the cliff. The moon is not yet sunk.
Full and bright, no need to grind or polish,
hanging in the black sky is my mind.
(Barnstone 2005, 204)

The moon in Buddhism is often an image for the enlightened mind, so he might seem to be writing symbolically. But I think he is also being literal to his experience. No longer separate from nature, his mind *is* the moon and the moon *is* his mind. Emerson might have said that Han Shan has become the transparent eyeball.

And yet Emerson especially among the Transcendentalists projected human concerns onto nature, drawing from the medieval trope of the Book of Nature, in which we can read God when we read nature spiritually. His transparent eyeball at such moments becomes the eye of a movie projector casting human thoughts on the screen of nature. It is this trope that Whitman echoes in one of his answers to a child's question, "What is the grass?"

Or I guess it is the handkerchief of the Lord,
A scented gift and remembrancer designedly dropped,
Bearing the owner's name someway in the corners, that we
may see and remark, and say Whose?

The grass is the flag of his cheerful disposition. It is the handkerchief of God. It is the child of vegetation. It is a "uniform hieroglyphic" of national unity in diversity. Or it is "the beautiful uncut hair of graves." But the grass is not the grass.

Han Shan, on the other hand, writes poems like the one above in which the full moon *is* his mind—he is the moon and the moon is him—yet he also questions such equivalences of the human with the natural. He questions the use of nature to symbolize human concerns instead of just being wholly what it is:

My heart is like the autumn moon
pure and bright in a green pool.
No, it's not like anything else.
How can I explain?
(Barnstone 2005, 200)

Han Shan's thought anticipates much modern and contemporary eco-poetry, such as Wallace Stevens's "The Snow Man," which says that "One must have a mind of winter" not to project human meaning on nature but to instead allow natural meanings to enter the mind, to become "the listener, who listens in the snow, / And, nothing himself, beholds / Nothing that is not there and the nothing that is" (Stevens, 9–10).

In *Republic of Apples, Democracy of Oranges*, such thought problems emerge in, for example, Xi Du's "Watching Crows at the Summer Palace." The poet makes the crows into a series of similes, each of which replaces the previous one with another human projection. Are they black-robed monks reciting sutras? Bills from hell requiring payment from humanity? Failed aspirations? He doesn't answer, but concludes:

> I know they will invade my dreams
> demanding words from me
> to praise the darkness.

Even these poems complaining about language, after all, are written in language. And if that language casts net after net but fails to capture the crow, then at least we can use our words to praise the darkness the crow manifests. This struggle to articulate a world that does not need words to have meaning, and that words inevitably distort, is central to much contemporary eco-poetry in China and America.

Daoist philosopher Zhuangzi wrote, "Words exist because of meaning; once you've gotten the meaning, you can forget the words. Where can I find a man who has forgotten words so I can have a word with him?" (Watson, 233). Perhaps we could talk with nature if we could just forget about words and talking. California poet Elena Karina Byrne writes in her prose poem in *Republic of Apples, Democracy of Oranges* that "Appropriation is the only conversation to have":

> Everyone is watching on shore, wind lost in its own white music. Or is it white noise? The kind of machine you buy so you can't hear your neighbor. You know, the one you heard through the hedge wall where hungry pigeons were breeding.

What is the white noise that keeps us from hearing the pigeons? Presumably it comes from the machine of the mind itself, which makes the human brain a lamp projecting onto nature instead of a mirror reflecting it. Presumably the noise is "the fence of language" that contemporary Chinese poet Sun Wenbo complains makes it impossible, in his poem "Nothing to Do with Crows," to truly see the crows because we "can't escape . . . consciousness."

Contemporary Mongolian poet Baoyinhexige's poem "Crows" also describes the doubleness of our appropriation of nature—how by projecting upon it we blind ourselves to its actuality. Thus, the poem declares the crows are utterly unaware of human respect and human hatred for them: they "do not even know / They are black." But the cross-species blindness goes both ways. The poem imagines the crows as patchers of the sky always flying and patching things up, and concludes that "people do not know / What it is they are patching." While it is tempting to answer that question as a reader, it is notable that the poet does not. He leaves the question resonating, unanswered, and perhaps unanswerable for anyone but a crow.

Wild Mind

Much contemporary eco-poetry comes from a sense that we have alienated ourselves from both nature and, ultimately, our humanity. In the West, this thought emerges in the Romantics with William Blake's "London," in which a river that is a "charter'd" sewer is produced by the same society that has fouled our lives and trapped us in "mind forg'd manacles." And it reappears in Gerard Manley Hopkins's elegy for nature in "God's Grandeur": "And all is seared with trade; bleared; smeared with toil;/And wears man's smudge and shares man's smell: the soil/Is bare now, nor can foot feel, being shod."

As antidote, Walt Whitman tells us, "This is what you shall do; Love the earth and sun and the animals [and] despise riches," and Emerson in "The American Scholar" writes that "Know Thyself" means to "Study Nature" and that nature's "laws are the laws of [your] own mind."

Thus, when eco-poet and Zen practitioner Gary Snyder says that "mind, imagination and language are...wild ecosystems" (1995, 168), he is echoing these earlier Western poets and how they think about healing the divide between nature and human nature.

However, it is not a stretch to state that, like some contemporary Chinese poets, Snyder is also echoing irascible Zen poets whose poems needle society's shallow concerns with wealth and power. For Han Shan, for example, living in this world is a kind of mental trap that we are too anthropocentric to comprehend:

> Like bugs in a bowl
> we all day circle, circle
> unable to get out.
> (Barnstone 2005, 205)

Trapped as we are within our own thought-systems, we too often see the living creatures with whom we share the planet in terms of their utilitarian value. The great Tang Dynasty poet Du Fu (712–770 CE) questions the carnivorous cycle, and even hints at a "deep ecology" in which we might imagine seeing animals and nature for what they are instead of what they mean to us.

> My young servant tied up a chicken to sell at market.
> Roped tight, the chicken struggled and squawked.
> My family hates seeing the chicken eating worms and ants,
> not knowing that once sold the chicken will be cooked.
> What's the difference between chickens and insects to a
>   human being?
> I scolded the servant and untied the chicken.
> I can never solve the problem of chickens and insects,
> so just lean against my mountain pavilion, gazing at the
>   cold river.
> (Barnstone 2005, 145)

If we see nature through the lens of utility, we reduce it to a resource. This disease of consciousness can undermine our humanity, too, when we think of others as resources. As Confucius says, "An honorable man is not a tool" (*Analect* 2:12).

Du Fu's poem foreshadows the poetry of Jane Hirshfield, whose work is steeped in Zen and Daoism. In "A Bucket Forgets Its Water," she implies that the human mind might be improved if it could only forget what filled it in the past and cease worrying about what will fill it in the future, holding "no grudges, fears / or regret." Better to be an empty bucket perhaps, not filled with language and emotion and social and political dreams and nightmares, like the Dao: "Dao is an empty vessel, / used without ever being filled" (Barnstone 2005, 14). Better to just be what we are, performing our function, the way a bucket conveys without thought or is useful even when empty:

> A bucket, upside down,
> is almost as useful as upright—
> step stool, tool shelf, drum stand, small table for lunch.

Here also Hirshfield echoes the *Dao De Jing,* which considers the usefulness of human tools to reside in their emptiness:

> Thirty spokes joined at one hub;
> emptiness makes the cart useful.
> Clay cast into a pot;
> the emptiness inside makes it useful.
> Doors and windows cut to make a room;
> emptiness makes the room useful.
> Thus, being is beneficial
> but usefulness comes from the void.
> (Barnstone 2005, 15)

Likewise, many of the Chinese and American eco-poets in *Republic of Apples, Democracy of Oranges* criticize the human obsession with usefulness, which turns the whole world into a tool: something to be used, a thing whose value lies in not being but making, not presence but something working towards an end, a list of things to accomplish before we kick the bucket.

Confucian Disobedience

What would the eco-poem written by a poet who is an empty, forgetful bucket, who has a wild mind, look like? It would not be an old-fashioned pastoral treating nature as a pathetic fallacy, or nature as a sign and set of symbols, or nature personified and given a voice. As John Shoptaw writes, "ecopoets cannot be naive about matters of perception and poetic representation, which are biologically and culturally specific (a bee's world is not a human's)." And yet eco-poems are written for humans, and with a didactic purpose: to teach us, to warn us, to humanize us, to reconnect us with our natural selves.

Sometimes the best way to achieve the didactic imperative in eco-poetry is by setting deep ecology aside and using a little old-fashioned personification. An example might be Sandra Alcosser's poem about pioneering environmentalist Rachel Carson, which begins, "1963 and the earth said *a little less poison please*." Her poem concludes,

> A little less 2-4-D—less DDT and BHC
> A little less in our well a little less in our bloodstream
> From the nerves of earthworm to the ovaries
> Of thrush and their exquisite melodies
> For everything eating and eaten—*a little less poison please*

We know that the earth is not speaking to us. How could it be? Yet the poem plays upon our knowledge of that fact to insist—nevertheless—that the earth is speaking to us. And the earth has a simple yet intensely moving message: "*a little less poison please.*"

Such messages would seem to be intuitively obvious, but when it is cheaper to pollute instead of conserving the earth and when the rollback of environmental standards meant to protect us is lauded as "reform" of "job-killing regulations," even simple environmental messages are deeply political (Semuels). The didactic mode of many of the American poems here would, therefore, seem to echo the Transcendentalists and their ideas of civil disobedience and nonconformity.

Ralph Waldo Emerson argued that to be spiritual, creative, and self-reliant, one must be a nonconformist, but it was his friend Thoreau who truly put those ideas into practice. Thoreau refused to pay the poll tax in protest of American imperialism and of the institution of slavery—a seminal act of civil disobedience that has inspired agents of social change from Gandhi to Martin Luther King Jr. to contemporary ecological activists. Like Melville's Bartleby the Scrivener, when Thoreau was confronted with participating in American materialist culture, he was willing to say, "I prefer not to."

Yet I would argue that to act in the American tradition of civil disobedience is similar to the Confucian retainer showing his loyalty by standing up to the ruler when that ruler is wrong—for the sake of the state and also to guide the ruler to rule ethically. As Confucius says in *Analect* 13.15, "If a ruler is evil and nobody opposes him, it could perhaps ruin the entire country." In fact, in "Civil Disobedience," Thoreau quotes Confucius in supporting his argument for civil action in protest of unethical government: "If a state is governed by the principles of reason, poverty and misery are subjects of shame; if a state is not governed by the principles of reason, riches and honors are the subjects of shame."

In Chinese poetic thought, such civil and ethical disobedience is a central role for the poet, one that goes all the way back to the third-century BCE poet Qu Yuan, who was sent into exile for honestly counseling his king. Qu Yuan drowned himself in protest, and his virtuous action is celebrated even today in the yearly Dragon Boat Festival. Many later Chinese poets took inspiration from Qu Yuan and stood up to mayors, kings, and emperors, risking their lives and livelihoods to do so. During the Beijing Spring and the Democracy Movement of the late 1970s and 1980s, the experimental poets of the Misty School risked exile and worse by composing poems of social protest. The current Chinese censorship of environmental documentaries and media reports of devastating Chinese pollution shows that it is still a dangerous thing to speak the inconvenient truth in China (Standaert, Mufson). Such censorship has taken root in the U.S. as well. The Environmental Protection Agency is currently run by petrofuel insiders who have stifled the free speech of ecological scientists, in order to undermine climate change research and to relax environmental regulation. Such insiders act on the unscientific theory of "hormesis," which asserts that exposure to toxins and radiation is actually good for one's health (Leber).

We see the Chinese and American poets in *Republic of Apples, Democracy of Oranges* speaking up—with the Cassandra call of devastating prophesy—in apocalyptic poems. In Suzanne Roberts's frighteningly funny "Apocalypse at the Safeway," people battle over the last can of tuna when it is announced that in the future you must "*eat only what you can grow.*" Brianna Lyn Sahagian-Limas's "To Burn a World" emerges from what Paul Boyer defines as the "prospect of global annihilation" that "filled the national consciousness" in the nuclear era, engendering a "bone-deep fear" (15). In her poem, Sahagian-Limas imagines apocalypse as a kind of erotic sparking and flaming between lovers that builds into a burning of the world with "warheads/and smokestacks," the heat "erasing everything/before we could explain." Her vision of nuclear annihilation as an orgasmic explosion of the human mind recalls William Carlos Williams. In "Asphodel, That Greeny Flower," he compares the bomb to "a flower," but one that will destroy us because we don't believe "that love/can so wreck our lives" (322).

Perhaps we don't believe in such "flower power" because it is hard to find spiritual solace in an environment that is increasingly urban and suburban, strip-mined and fracked. The China of today is not the China of Wang Wei. Zheng Xiaoqiong's "Industrial Zone" bemoans the way even light is unnatural in the human-built environment: "The white light is on, the building is lit, the machine is on,/my fatigue is lit, the blueprint is lit." In the lit city, the people are "weak and homesick," missing their spiritual home in nature.

At the same time, the moon continues to light the world with its full emptiness: "the moonlight is on, a full hollow of emptiness, the lychee tree is lit,/a breeze blows the clear emptiness in its body while silence keeps/its year-round quietness, only insects sing in the bushes." The moonlight somehow still has its power to "light up" the narrator's "falling heart." The moon and stars are still up there, after all, beyond the city's light pollution and smog, hanging in the sky like Han Shan's mind.

Cultural ideas of the sort shared by the poets in *Republic of Apples, Democracy of Oranges* seek to catalyze a shift in consciousness towards a more sustainable way of being in the world. They seek to be a cure to the sort of infected consciousness that Kevin Prufer warns us about in "An American Tale": "cultural ideas" that are "a kind of virus. Violence, terror, fascism/incubate inside a host mind/that passes them on to other/susceptible minds." As William Carlos Williams cautions us in his atom bomb poem, "Asphodel, That Greeny Flower":

> If a man die
>> it is because death
>>> has first
> possessed his imagination.
> (334)

Violence comes from violent thought, from the little exploding atom bomb inside the brain. As Einstein wrote, "The unleashed power of the atom has changed everything save our modes of thinking, and thus we drift toward unparalleled catastrophe. We shall require a substantially new manner of thinking if mankind is to survive." And to begin changing how we think, we might learn from the great Chinese poets to see ourselves as part of nature and each other instead of separate, and to look at human concerns with a certain detached humor.

Gary Snyder is the most prominent eco-poet of his generation, and has stood in for many others in this introduction in part because of his deep immersion in Asian literature and religion. However, it is important to note that he is not an anomaly. Asian spiritual critiques of society deeply influenced a wide range of American writers during the era of the Beat, Deep Image, and Black Mountain poets. It is Ginsberg declaiming, "We're not our skin of grime, we're not dread bleak dusty imageless locomotives, we're golden sunflowers inside" (106), and James Wright caressing a pony in Minnesota and knowing that if he steps out of his body he "will break into blossom" (57). As I write elsewhere,

> For James Wright, the Chinese poets seemed "to have saved their souls in the most violent circumstances," so that for us, in a time when our "imaginations have been threatened with numbness and our moral beings are nearly shattered by the moral ghastliness of public events and private corporations," the Chinese poets retain an "abiding radiance," they are a kind of salvation. (Barnstone, 2003)

Asian literature gave Wright and succeeding generations of American authors a tradition of ethical poetry that connects to nature and questions the values of a society driven by money, competition, exploitation, and power.

It's true that their revolutionary poetic consciousness, like that of many contemporary political and ecological poets, was equally inspired by the American Transcendentalists that we discussed earlier. Yet the fact that the Transcendentalist tradition is itself cribbed from the Asian spiritual and philosophical tradition suggests a startling conclusion: all American eco-poetry is also Pacific Rim poetry at the root.

ACKNOWLEDGEMENT

The inspiration for this anthology of American and Chinese eco-poetry emerged from a Luce Initiative on Asian Studies and the Environment grant to Whittier College. As part of this grant, Chinese and American writers participated in an exchange of visits to each other's countries, involving lectures, readings, class visits, and other public events at Beijing Normal University, the Lu Xun Academy, Yunnan University, Whittier College, Santa Monica College, and Pomona College. For their work in making this exchange possible, we especially thank Ming Di; Jason Carbine, Director of the Luce grant program at Whittier College; and Denise Wong Velasco, Administrative Coordinator of the grant. We also thank Jason Carbine and the Luce Foundation for financial support in publishing this issue.

SOURCES

Barnstone, Tony. "Letters from Dead Friends." Perihelion 6:3, 2003, http://www.webdelsol.com/Perihelion/barnstone.htm.

Barnstone, Tony and Chou Ping, eds., *The Anchor Book of Chinese Poetry: From Ancient to Contemporary, The Full 3000-Year Tradition*. New York: Anchor, 2005.

Barnstone, Tony and Chou Ping, eds. and trans. *The Art of Writing: Teachings of the Chinese Masters*. Boulder, CO: Shambhala, 1996.

Barnstone, Willis, Tony Barnstone, and Xu Haixin, eds. and trans. *Laughing Lost in the Mountains: Selected Poems of Wang Wei*. Lebanon, NH: University Press of New England, 1991.

Boyer, Paul. *By the Bomb's Early Light: American Thought and Culture at the Dawn of the Atomic Age*. New York: Pantheon Books, 1985.

Einstein, Albert. Telegram on behalf of the Emergency Committee of Atomic Sciences to several hundred prominent Americans.

Ginsberg, Allen. *Collected Poems: 1947–1997*. New York: Harper Collins, 2010.

Leber, Rebecca. "The EPA's Bold New Idea Has Massive Implications for Public Health." *Mother Jones,* 3 October 2018 12:48 p.m., https://www.motherjones.com/environment/2018/10/the-epas-bold-new-idea-massive-implications-public-health/

Lewis, Todd and Kent Bicknell. "The Asian Soul of Transcendentalism." *Educating about Asia,* 16:2 (fall 2011): 12–19.

Mufson, Steven. "This Documentary Went Viral in China. Then It Was Censored. It Won't Be Forgotten." *Washington Post.* 16 March 2015, https://www.washingtonpost.com/news/energy-environment/wp/2015/03/16/this-documentary-went-viral-in-china-then-it-was-censored-it-wont-be-forgotten/?utm_term=.e5dc4868501c/

Semuels, Alana. "Do Regulations Really Kill Jobs?" *The Atlantic.* 19 January 2017, https://www.theatlantic.com/business/archive/2017/01/regulations-jobs/513563/

Shoptaw, John. "Why Ecopoetry? There's No Planet B." Poetry Foundation, 4 January 2016, www.poetryfoundation.org/poetrymagazine/articles/70299/why-ecopoetry/

Snyder, Gary. *A Place in Space: Ethics, Aesthetics and Watersheds.* Berkeley: Counterpoint, 1995.

Snyder, Gary. *The Practice of the Wild.* Berkeley: Counterpoint, 2010.

Standaert, Michael. "As It Looks to Go Green, China Keeps a Tight Lid on Dissent." YaleEnvironment360, 2 November 2017, https://e360.yale.edu/features/as-it-looks-to-go-green-china-keeps-a-tight-lid-on-dissent/

Stevens, Wallace. *The Collected Poems of Wallace Stevens.* New York: Vintage, 1990.

Watson, Burton. *The Complete Works of Zhuangzi.* New York: Columbia University Press, 2013.

Wei, Qingqi. "Chinese Ecocriticism in the Last Ten Years." *The Oxford Handbook of Ecocriticism,* ed. Greg Garrard. England: Oxford University Press, 2014.

Williams, William Carlos. *The Collected Poems of William Carlos Williams: 1939–1962.* Volume 2. New York: New Directions, 1991.

Wright, James. *The Branch Will Not Break: Poems.* Middletown, CT: Wesleyan University Press, 1959.

Bamboo, Orange, Ocean, and Beyond————————————

The oldest Chinese poem is a very short one with eight words only, two in four pairs, roughly translated into English like this:

Cut a bamboo	断竹
Tie the ends	续竹
Shoot a mud	飞土
And chase that meat	逐肉

In its straightforward description of the early hunting days when our ancestors were making bows from bamboo trees, we see how humans were destroying nature, as well as how smart they were in using bamboo branches to make a bow; we see how they captured animals and consumed their meat. From the earliest days of literature, nature poems were anti-nature; that is, about how opposed to nature human actions were. Later poets tried to sing of how beautiful nature was, but their words paled in the light of their cruelty in killing and eating other creatures.

The difference betwcen nature poetry and eco-poetry seems to be the awareness, in the latter, of human nature: how we destroy the balance of the natural world around us. Part of the awareness results in an attempt to reinterpret the earlier poems. Why were there human voices in the deep, quiet forest in Wang Wei's "Deer Enclosure"? Why was sunset reflected on the green moss? Was it a beautiful scene for Wang Wei or horrible deforestation? The awakening sense of ecology is also seen in reevaluating our daily life, as Duo Duo writes in his poem "Gratitude": "In returning what we've taken, we take again." Duo Duo criticizes everything we do today to despoil nature, from mining to drilling to cutting down trees. Yet we imagine ourselves to be "singers of the earth"—in singing, we forget for a brief moment our sinful actions. Singers or sinners, we are part of what we simultaneously enjoy and destroy. But we also see how small we are: a chrysanthemum, an oriole, a croaker. We are mixed into nature, as Song Wei suggests in his poem "Small Notes in My Old Age":

> I return to the village and see lots of red peppers
> sunbathing on the threshing floor with me

Xi Du expresses something similar in his poem "Seabirds" but with a broader perspective—the land and sea and living creatures and even things we build all responding to each other:

Sometimes the sea meanders to the land, folded as a seagull.
Sometimes the land walks to the sea, hiding in a boat.
The sea and land go deeper to each other through rain and lightning.
. . . .
while crowds of white-robed monks rush to the sunrise

It is probably in this holistic view of the world that we feel less guilty of being a destructive and consumerist human, seeing ourselves as plants, birds, rain, and even "fifty-year-old dust" with feathers and wings, as Zhang Qinghua says in his poem "Dozing at Middle Age." That's how contemporary Chinese poets see themselves— instead of anthropomorphizing other species.

Another interesting feature of eco-poetry is the awareness of geography. Ancient poets name localities in their poems; later poets talk only vaguely about villages and rivers. In returning to the ancient tradition, contemporary Chinese poets are writing about their hometowns, or where they live and work. For instance, Song Wei writes about his hometown, Muchun, in Sichuan province; Gu Ma writes about a small town on the ancient Silk Road in northwest China; Li Suo writes about Kashgar, where she grew up; Jike Bu about Cold Mountains, where she has spent all her life; Lü De'an about a small village by the Ocean Corner where he lived; Jiang Hao about Hainan, the South Sea Island; Duo Duo, even more specifically, about the White Sand Gate in the South Sea Island, where he migrated to; Li Heng, who moves around, writes about "almost-no-town." There is an old saying in Chinese, "every mountain raises one kind of person, and so does every river." For example, in Yu Xiaozhong's poem we feel the River Qi disposition, and in Zhang Er's the Buji River temperament.

In China, poets are not just poets but mountain poets, river poets, urban poets, or poets of the grassland. And they are not just any mountain poets or any river poets, but poets of specific mountains and rivers with names. Huang Bin is known for writing of his Shennongjia Mountains, and Yang Ke for his Flower Mountain in southern China. It is in this sense that locating them, as we do in the back of this collection, becomes meaningful: if you know a little bit of the geography of China (and the U.S. as well) or if you look up places on a map, you understand the poets better.

Ancient Chinese poets were poets of geography and traveled no less than we do today. Anyone reading Li Bai (701–762) cannot escape noticing the Yangtze River, literally the "Long River" in Chinese. The best known of his poems about the river is "Seeing Off Meng Haoran for Guangling at Yellow Crane Tower." In it, he describes traveling on the Yangtze to the Kingdom of Chu, and meeting a local poet, who later departs eastward along the river to Yangzhou (Guangling):

My old friend bids farewell to Yellow Crane Tower,
traveling east to Yangzhou in the flowery March.
His lonely sail, a distant shadow. Blue sky fades,
only the Long River flows, flows to the far horizon.

Li Bai mentions over sixty rivers and eighty mountains in his poems. Du Fu (712–770), we see in his poetry, traveled even more. In fact, almost all the ancient Chinese poets and writers were travelers or migrants. The very first book in China's history, *The Book of Mountains and Seas* (山海经), is a series of volumes containing geographies as well as mythologies and polytheistic religions, with detailed descriptions of places inside China and beyond, including places in the Americas.

Hopefully, readers will remember some poets in this anthology by noticing the locality they write about—a river, a mountain, or a detail about where they live or have lived. But of course this collection cannot be a complete mapping of poets who write eco-poetry, but only the writing available at the time of publication. Mapping, mapping, mapping. Without drawing a map, Columbus couldn't have reached America. Without describing the mountains and seas in *The Book of Mountains and Seas,* migrating Asians couldn't have arrived in America and become the Indigenous people. Gary Snyder's "Turtle Island" says as much. The earliest Chinese words were carved into the bones of sea turtles, and these bones were used as oracles. Like the land that drifts slowly in the oceans for eons, turtles have long lives. Eco-poetry is a new perception of where we live, what's underneath us, what's around, and what's above. Hai Zi wrote "Asia Bronze" in 1984 to rebel against Misty poetry, which was much influenced by Western literature. The poem brought huge attention to Hai Zi and awakened an affirmation of the land beneath us, the bronze-colored soil of Asia. And our darker skin. The poem was perhaps the first eco-poem in contemporary China. However, eco-poetry is not limited by local borders, but presents a cosmic perspective, extending from where we are standing to wherever our imaginations take us. Beyond ocean and sky, even to the moon, which Hai Zi tells us Qu Yuan and other poets reached. Jiang Hao, in his poem "The Shape of the Ocean," writes:

When you ask me what the ocean's shape is like
I should bring you two sacks full of sea water.
They are the ocean's shape, like two eyes,
or what the ocean seems like because of a pair of eyes.

I always think of this poem's title and wonder if the oceans separate the land into continents, or if the land separates water into oceans. From South China and Taiwan to Southwest China, traveling along the Yangtze River, then west and north before winding down to the East Sea, and from there crossing the Pacific (flying over many islands), traveling eastward to California, and with many turns to America's East Coast, then crossing the Atlantic to Europe and back to Asia—words migrate like birds.

Migration is a normal pattern of contemporary life, as it was in ancient times. What's fascinating about eco-poetry is what it reveals about archaeology and anthropology, in addition to geography. The human-shaped scripts in Yang Ke's poem "Walking towards Flower Mountain" are the earliest writings of the Zhuang people in Guangxi, southern China.

> From the tip of a boar's tusk I came
> From a pheasant's fluffed-up feathers I came
> From strange power of bone ornaments I came

Ethnic minority culture is an important component of this gathering of eco-poetry, as seen, for example, in the work of Aku Wuwu, Jidi Majia, and Jike Bu, a member of the younger generation of Yi poets. In her poem, she sings about Suoma, a woman in the Cold Mountains region:

> Love her—love her breathtaking color
>   from blooming,
> the traces she left
> in the wind the rain the scorching sun.
> Nothing disdains her beauty: she is pure
> like ice jade
> but she is not just pretty and frail.
> Her sonorous voice comes from the air,
> the revolving stream, the soil.

With the rise of eco-poetry, ethnic poets in China have begun to promote their cultures and languages, including their own writing systems. This is one difference between them and the Han majority poets, who write in Chinese and are concerned with reinventing a poetic form. For example, what strikes me in the first reading of Li Sen's "Orange in the Wilderness" is its three or four characters in each line, resembling the style used in the *Book of Songs*, the first collection of poems from the eleventh to sixth centuries BCE in China.

> sun rises in southeast
> orange in wilderness
> yellow in orange
> sunshine in orange
> shadow in orange
> orange next to orange
> orange on the roof

Another example of a search for fresh forms is "The Thirty-three tributaries of the Lancang River in Nanping County, Yunnan province" by Lei Pingyang (not included here). The poem was hugely controversial when it was first published in 2002, as it did little more than name each tributary and its length. Is it a poem or not? It doesn't have adjectives or verbs, but just names and numbers and the directions the rivers flow. But with its similar spirit to the style of *The Book of Mountains and Seas,* it is the rediscovery of an ancient way of writing. It's as informative as school textbooks, which reminds me of Marianne Moore's "Poetry" (1924): "nor is it valid /to discriminate against 'business documents and/school-books.'" It is also the very nature of detailed descriptions of things in Moore's poetry that makes her a pioneer eco-poet. She writes in "Sea Unicorns and Land Unicorns":

> With their respective lions—
> "mighty monoceroses with immeasured tayles"—
> . . . .
> the long keel of white exhibited in tumbling,
> disperses giant weeds
> and those sea snakes whose forms, looped in the foam,
>   "disquiet shippers."

What surprises me most is the "monoceros" at the beginning of this poem, which I interpret as the Monoceros (Latin: "unicorn") constellation that parallels with the unicorns. This is why I see in some American poets the holistic perspectives of ancient Chinese, who look at the land, the sea, and the constellations above in forming their mythologies of what's around us and beyond.

Yangtze Overlook, Xiling Gorge, 2000.
Photograph by Linda Butler.

Xiling Gorge is forty-seven miles long.
The Three Gorges Dam is near its
eastern end. This upstream view
includes a farmhouse with a satellite
dish—a luxury that was rarely seen
in rural areas before 2000—and
a new highway (at left).

AKU WUWU

Four Poems

RED-FRUITED HAWTHORN

Treading the fallen leaves,
I returned to Salem.
Before my arrival,
the autumn wind
had taken away all this year's leaves
from the trees.

Left are all the red berries
shining with a naked brightness.
All the poison juices of the body
make the sunlight of this town surprisingly
piercing.

The people in Salem
planted trees bearing poisonous fruits
merely out of appreciation,
desiring a kind of
poison-rich beauty.

WOLF SKIN

At an Indian folklife festival,
a white man in Indian array of wolf skin,
was dancing sincerely around a sacred drum.
I could not ask him
whether he had any Indian blood
for he seemed too solemn and stately.

An old Indian man nearby told me
in a plain deep voice
as long as one puts on a wolf skin he
is either our enemy
or one of our folk.
A wolf is the animal
hurting us the most and is
also a divine animal
we always worship.

Neither an enemy of the Indians,
nor their fellow folk,
yet, longed to
put on the magic Indian wolf skin.

Suddenly,
in the center of the wolf skin
I spotted
a small
bullet hole.

AVENGING DEER

In North America
deer and humans
enjoy the same modern civilization.

In the daytime, deer live in
fertile meadows
and tranquil woods.

At night they always want to go to town
to hear rock and roll
to see happy people.

The entire city
except for houses of different styles and
the magnificent churches
is but a patchwork of meadow,
and deer rush in from the four directions.

Deer, desirous of civilization,
deer, to ascertain the meaning of civilization
speak for, search for an eternal road
rushing towards the ever-pale highway
under the moon.

The spurring cars
help deer realize their dreams
without exception.

At dawn, on the meadows along the highway,
the deer draw pictures
with their frozen bodies
that even God above cannot see.

My memory flashes back to the Yi lands,
to those who regain dignity by
paying the price with their life,
hurting their enemy by hurting themselves;
those daring avengers face death unflinchingly,
those innocents akin to suicidal deer.
My heart knows those deer too
are groups of avengers.

In those moments before dawn,
the wounded souls of those
avenging deer
rush to nearby towns and villages
with those magnificent and mysterious churches.

GRASS EFFIGY

In the mountain hamlets,
those who know how to make
the tied grass effigies,
who know how to do the grass effigy rituals,
number more than the ant eggs beneath the stone slabs.
Thus, in expanses big or small
of forest
below the village
sown there by seeds from airplanes
the trees seem like bunches of spiders
carrying their eggs,
seem like married women in the fields
carrying their children as they plant.

But, in the mountain hamlets,
when children cry within the home,
and the cuckoo calls without,
then cries of those "pine tree children"
day by day turn to duff;
and for this, four seasons of the year,
the sounds of the wind in the pine forests,
grows ever greener.

And though people have ears,
they don't hear it;
and though they have eyes,
they don't see it.

Once the effigies were ritually sent off,
the matron of the family felt things were safe.
But, when the hearth fire verbosely crackled,
the agitated matron
withdrew the half-burnt sticks,
then stuck them into the water within
the hog slop trough.

Not long after,
the brother of the matron of the home slipped along the way,
falling into and drowning within the waters.
This bad news was spread by the wind,
and her laments were like putting
cold water on a fire to kill it.

The red-footed grass is cut and grows,
is cut and grows;
The grass effigies in the pine forests—
the old are followed by the new,
the old are followed by the new…
In the past, among the twelve sons of snow
were the red-footed grasses, among the sons of snow.
But not many people remember much of this anymore.
Now ant eggs have become stars in the sky,
becoming the old bear's most lovely ornaments.

Translations by Mark Bender

Five Poems

THE HORSE AND THE HOLY MAN

Spirit is not in the I, but between I and thou. It is not like the blood that circulates in you, but like the air in which you breathe. Martin Buber

The stable shadows indigo as the boy strokes
The neck of his beloved that coats
His hand with a must of sweat and leather
The dappled gray leans into the pressure
While the boy in the red riding habit pours
Peppery oats into a manger
Then large teeth with small scratches from grazing
Begin to chew inside its sensitive lips

What better expresses beauty of the inner
Than infant tenderness toward another—
I have watched two alone in a pasture
Whicker, exchanging weathers
No longer beasts, no longer orphan beings—
They breathe into the nostrils of each other

WINGED HUSSARS

Once we wore swan feathers—
Eagle Vulture Ostrich Goose.

O the beauty of our fear—

Winged Hussars charged toward us
Toward us and through.

We wore cymbals and feathers
To make ourselves bigger
To deafen the others—

Fear snaps like a banner.
Fear chatters. Like now. Like footfall.
Like clatter. I hear
A heart coming for me, charging through
The vestibule, charging through
The bony labyrinth of my ear.

GOD   THE CONDOR

I pull the God of Thunder I pull Him
From a nest I pull a little nestling limp

Hold Him to my chest from His stomach take
Half a cup of plastic half a cup of glass
And from His crop lift four bottle caps
What will make us well again what will make
Us sing poisoned by ideas poisoned by machines
God is cleaning up now God is eating

Inside a clown-pink face lead bullet casings
A black boa frames His shoulders like a painting
Imagine no more soaring no more Pleistocene
No more clouds pulled together by His wingbeats

God's coming for us now He looks a little queasy
He rubs his head against the rock He sharpens His beak

MOTHERS

From under water and under tar,
Down from the walls of caves
They came The biologist made
A circle with her arms
That calf's heart must have weighed
Twenty-five pounds she said. *Deep inside*
Each bison there is a bible,
Otherwise how could they survive
Our bullets and cliffs
Our cities and flames
Our soups simmering
With the heads of their babies
Each mother grazes patiently—
A ton of flesh made of grass blades

1963

1   PRESIDENTS AND PREMIERS ADDRESS THE YOUNG
LADIES OF THE SEMINARY FROM OUTER SPACE

Birds shimmy seeds into topknots of trees
Beget strangler figs dangling toward gravity
To shelter the seminary

Who sit in a circle of white pleats
And blue blazers and listen to their leaders'
Voices from outer space preaching—
Mutually assured destruction by land or sea

Who will they rocket next—a chimpanzee
Fruit flies, a dog they snatch from the street
We cultivate anomie—roaring at reality
With its roots in *everything the king can see*

One girl lacquers her hair into a torpedo

Who can we believe? We girls of the seed
Bed, we—young ladies of the seminary

2   I HAD JUST COME TO TERMS WITH FALLOUT, AND ALONG
COMES RACHEL CARSON (CARTOON IN *SATURDAY REVIEW*)

1963 and the earth said *a little less poison please*
With rustling sounds through fallen leaves
The sparrows flitting understory
Said yes please less for me—the ant hoisting
His brother's body in the nest said yes
And sharks feeding in the sea and fish eagles
Building cribs of mops and lawn chairs yes
And vultures who couldn't stop eating
Could not stop eating

A little less 2-4-D—less DDT and BHC
A little less in our well a little less in our bloodstream
From the nerves of earthworm to the ovaries
Of thrush and their exquisite melodies
For everything eating and eaten—*a little less poison please*

Eating Fish

I eat fish for breakfast
I eat fish for lunch
I eat fish for dinner
I eat fish most every day
For when I don't I soon begin to itch
Ah Jing said, "I ate Ah Mi's mom."
Been years since they threw her ashes into the Pacific
Just think of all the fish I have eaten from that sea
Every one delicious
Fish scales scintillate
But when a fish dies that flash disappears, becomes flesh
A flash I love to eat
Whenever Ah Mi eats fish she thinks of her mom
Even wrote a poem on the subject, which makes me think of mine
I think of both our moms
And sometimes other moms as well
Ah Mi's mom
Has her soul been on my tongue?
And what of those saltier than souls
Those flashes with a delicate distinction
Yet still my thoughts return to
Mom
Lying in that hospital ward
In a year or two I may well be eating her
And Ah Mi will be too
And Ah Jing and Ah Liao and Ah Tun and Ah Fa and Ah Han and
    Ah Cui
And all the others who are not so Ah
But love to eat fish
We'll all be eating fish one day
"Mmm," we'll say. "So savory"

Translation by Steve Bradbury

Crows

Crows do not know
That people believed in them.
Crows do not know that
Later, people hated them.

And even more so,
Crows do not know
Why this is so.

The Mayor of Tokyo
Once called upon the public
To use crows as cooking fare
Yet not one cook
Was tempted to do so.

Crows do not even know
They are black.

Crows are the numerous patchers of the sky
Patching endlessly and flying ceaselessly
And people do not know
What it is they are patching.

Translation by Mark Bender

Two Poems

A DIALECTIC TREATISE

The sun has burned out its core and appears now as a flaming coin
The type with the center punched out, the ones my grandfather
    smuggled back from Vietnam
The negation of space is in actuality a space itself
The man at the counter asks for coffee without cream
The waitress says they are out of cream, is milk okay
The man instead asks for coffee without milk
The ground in the forest of the city is full of potholes
The tower stumps have already been smelted
The statues built from their ingots feel like Ozymandias must have
The wonders we beheld the day before were overnight transformed
    into minimalist monoliths
The postmodernist's death threat to anything resembling a firm stance
The cuckoo's nest is sitting vacant, though not for lack of demand
The tea kettle screams for attention on the induction stove
The excited space within plays the opening of Beethoven's 9th
The Hegelians are discussing the duality of the void and the object
The negative denouncer doesn't get the irony
The void becomes manifest and devours the critical edge of the cinema
The weekend box office is through the roof now that we don't have
    to believe anything
The fantasies I've created have more agency than my reality does
The one where she bit clean through my neck seems to speak
    for itself the most

WHATEVER REMAINS OF LEON CZOLGOSZ

Boardwalk lost its property value when the water kept rising
Past projections assumed we could continue on like this
Ronald Reagan mistook his jelly beans for the nuclear football
Consensus is he's bringing back patriotism
Dread is the consensus on our side of the fence
Nothing seems to matter when there is no future
Future projections stop assuming anything
Imagining an alternative feels like a mental exercise reserved for
Fringe academics who secretly fear their criticism is fueling the fire
Thinking seems like a luxury not afforded to caged animals
Rats run on a wheel for lower wages than hamsters
Prey is easiest to take if it imagines itself on top
Dead time is the rhythm of repetitive brain injury
Calendars read: work, procreate, and pay your taxes

This: Beside the Arno

for Paula and William Merwin

Alive while one more island friend heads skyward
with thinned wings—her bereft
may ask who is her ragged Virgil now, or who is his

says his own tomb will read: *Valley Spirit*—blind
seer solo in his garden now, held his late wife's hand,
he's certain, were they asleep, was the hand warm, and

then metal chill, what ill wind wore the cape of care?
Come, she will.
Yet, a garden.   Come, it may.   Come it will.

—Alive, while she headed for skies with ragged
wings. I was married once on such a winter-still
day of Ides. Now solo in verdigris, seeding the sun

Now husbands alone in their gardens   Now wives in
their skies or beds   I—on the banks of rivers
and mirrors.

Now, an elder perched in the un-worded
un-nameable rubble of his once marriage bed in
bombed Aleppo lists to music truer than my words.

Now, the Fascists have come to power sleekly
as the river rats. Will there be an April? Come she
will. Alive while blood-suns lower where they swim—

where a yesterday moon mounts a river's glass
where the long-tailed rats sleek-skim currents between
a last light's hammered silver chains.   Jewels?   Spirits?

Necklaces? Ides? Only shine.   Only another
prophecy has passed. Then may the poets turn
to gardeners.   Their small will   be done.

BRUCE BOND

Two Poems

ECO

The other member of this conversation
is the forest we are in, the one that is here

and not quite here, not the woods we knew
when we were young and lost and elsewhere.

I too have a new face and the faceless wound
it floats on, the long loneliness for power

to salvage some broken friend or ocean.
Just when I thought I was alone again,

my limbs take on the look of skies on fire,
as planets do, and monks, and drunken men

whose vague unease is longing to be shared.
Even the best convictions dream the damaged

world that says, I know, I too am worried.
The other voice among us is a certain change

in the wind. And once, when I was young,
I heard it speak. And in its speaking, listen.

ATOLL

The shovels of the last war here
       take on, in time, a phantom life.

All night the slough of rock, steel,
       unclaimed bone, the dull heft

and pallor of silt, raised, turned,
       released, and raised again as dust.

An island buries what it must.
       Long after the ash has settled

over the eyes, after the suns on flags
       have burned and longboats resume,

casting their nets across the wreckage,
       the spades keep doing what

spades do. The ghost in the machine
       of an otherwise peaceful life

worries the earth, burying the dead
       in the dead who just keep rising.

Which is why the islanders leave their home
       in foreign hands, promised

for their absence the refinement
       of a weapon to end all weapons,

to bomb the hell out of heaven
       and give it back. And shipped off

into exile for good, tented on a near shore
  with a crate of provisions,

the ocean breeze their only contract,
  they see it: the blooming of suns

that stretch their haloes from the target.
  Twenty-three in all, each

with its prevailing wind. They feel the heat
  on their faces. And in their eyes,

the image of earth, beyond reach
  or recognition, scattered to the open sea.

Zoo Prayers

Everyone who is born holds dual citizenship, in the kingdom of the well and in the kingdom of the sick. Although we all prefer to use only the good passport, sooner or later each of us is obliged, at least for a spell, to identify ourselves as citizens of that other place. Susan Sontag

1

Benign. Be well. Be born. Be night, be
nothing. Be not darkness or at least be
dusk, Arkansas waving goodbye to the day
as it does with an indigo sky. Benign. Be
nope, be not yet, be a night for
sleeping, for love, for morning
surely there. Be crepuscular, pacing
early, up with the black rhino
at this zoo, how astounding the only
of his species all the way down here
rises with the first fog though there is no
other of his kind to teach him so.
Be the highway humming not far
from his enclosure—the ceaseless crease
of hurry, all those on their way to work
except me. Be the hiss of his urine on the hay,
the steam rising. Be his caretakers.
They say, *Morning, Jo,* and arrive
with treats, reaching their hands into
the soft womb of his open mouth.

2

Benign. Be the birds. Or better,
the bear—the old grizzly—rising too.
Though it's December she isn't
hibernating today. Besides, she hasn't
smelled the crisp of real
winter since her mother was shot;
she was a cub then, drugged and packed
in the back of a pickup across the Delta
to here. She is nearly thirty-five now, her
slop of spit thick, her white tongue
licking her reflection in the plexiglass,
perhaps all she knows. Oh, and she knows,
she can see it from her cage: That traffic
never stops. Especially at this hour, the rush
edging this zoo. I ask her: What do you make
of that ceaseless static, that almost-ocean
sound, that exhaust carried by the stiff breeze?
Do you understand the direction of those streams
of lights—one flowing white, the other red—
one headed your way, the other already gone?
Or is it true what I read, that once an animal knows
something is not a threat, to that animal the thing
disappears?

3

The other question is this: Will that happen
once I get the news if this cancer is
not a cancer at all? Will I forget what it is to be
this close to it? And can that lonely
orangutan about to die
from cancer herself be told? Today I can't tell
if she plays hide-and-seek
under a bed sheet or if she's trying to pull
that white cloth up over her flat face to
go away from here; she raises her arms
like the mighty oaks they are, dripping
with the Spanish moss of her fur.
Her pelvis is extended, and I've been told:
the zoo expects she only has a few weeks.
Can she see the grief on my face?
Or does she notice me at all? Am I rudely
gawking too long, or worse, just another
spectator, already disappeared?

Surely the drivers on the other side don't
think of this dying ape, imagine what's
caged behind that stand of bamboo. Certainly
they don't know they're inhaling the loud yellow
roar the old grizzly just let out, don't think
to turn down their car radios enough
to hear that otherworldly echo of
siamang gibbons, a loud throbbing
I can hear clear to the other side of this park,
a clean, ululating howl
beat from the stretch of their ballooning
bullfrog throats.

4

With my fingers hooked in the chain
link, I taste the high-fructose squabble
of countless rainbow lorikeets, and later,
with a quarter in a red slot machine,
I catch a palm's worth of feed
meant to tempt the searching barbels
of countless koi, coax their sex-wet
mouths up to the dangerous air to kiss
my fingertips. I squat near the pond,
and like the crazy lady I've become,
I talk to the fish, tell them I was once
a driver on that highway, know what it is
not to know to look. The bird-bright
carp answer me with tiny round
pops and splashes, their hungry sounds,
bodies of every color of fire
slap and fight for food. Again, if I enter
the kingdom of the well once more,
will I drive that highway ready to
get where I'm going, forget my time done
on the other side of this fence?

5

At another exhibit, an elephant
so old her face is practically
a skull covered in skin freckled pink
sways and sways, a self-soothing sign.
I have stood so long watching
her that her keeper feels sorry for me,
I can tell. He takes me back to meet
his elephant, says, *This old girl used to log*
a camp in Burma, pulled trees out
of the ground with her trunk. She's sly
and can contract the veins
in her big ears to avoid a needle when
the vet comes. The man uses a giant
hook to bend the colossal
knee, shows me the vast
desert on the bottom of her foot.
I reach down, place one finger inside
a deep trench, think: My God,
here is the impossible—
this parched land, like Mars
maybe but gray, the terrible rage
long burned out. Or maybe
more like the seas of the moon,
tides of dry powder-like rock,
this other world hidden all along
underneath my own. Quietly,
so only the elephant with her
big, sly ears can hear,
I say, *I am ready, Lord. Okay.*
Take me there.

ELENA KARINA BYRNE

Two Poems

WE WERE WASTE AND WELTER THERE IN THE DAY: FACEBOOK

The universe is the ultimate free lunch. Alan Guth

Appropriation is the only conversation to have. I dream the same
wave is breaking over me, aqua alga bloom. Everyone is watching on
shore, wind lost in its own white music. Or is it white noise? The kind
of machine you buy so you can't hear your neighbor. You know, the one
you heard through the hedge wall where hungry pigeons were breeding.
Who can blame your theft for feeling? Come to me, dear thousand friends,
I do not know: I will share. Cockle and critical mass and tracking our electrons
from unruly kingdoms of north and south in the black hole's spinning top,
Newton on the way to the store, with shorthand flurry and fleeing from . . .
America's imaginative engagement is sex and war, unverifiable claim what
cannot be in the stash cash. Looks like me in your photo. Looks like a motion ago
was expulsion, dull dish rebrand again. Costume cosmic context in the music
silenced in the bushes. I don't even know what it sounds like in my own closet
when closed in and alone. Faith here fails its own science, is an art argument
with thrown bread, blood puddings and dining chairs, the petted dead,
quicklime, pollution and a plum for the sleeping eye. Welcome now. Welcome . . .

HOME FILLED WITH THOUSANDS OF FLOWERS,

      so many flowers you couldn't breathe coming in
the front door, rising lilac-bruised and picked and plucked fresh,
slipping on hothouse skins, hot-headed-red over green, in spring's
temper tantrum in silence for this . . . wedding funeral, constellation-
petals large and small, stem and stamen, torn softly, each
severed pink and yellow head where the missing bed is now,
missing moon table and chairs replaced with so many flower-mouths,
but see, there over the fireplace mantle is its invisible family portrait, all
impatiens over peony, the private parts of field lavender chained
      around the ankles of the children no longer here.
Bathtub filled with so many avoidable sunflowers, long names in herb rows,
thousand mouse corsage, dust lintel and moldings, greening their perfume,
still wet in prayer along the stained corridor, snail trails and seed nails
      driven away from ground, wearing early widow's weeds—
what will happen to you when you sleep in the house, now
      Anemone-naked, its roof gone?

CHEN DONGDONG

Light Up

Light up an oil lamp in the rocks so they can see
the sea. Let them see
the sea and the antique fish.
See the light too,
a lamp held high on the hill.

Light up a lamp in the streams so they can see
the live fish. Let them see
the fish and the silent sea.
See the sunset as well,
a firebird flying up from the trees.

Light up all the lamps. When I block the north wind
with my hands and stand between two canyons,
I think they will all gather around me
and see I speak a language
like a lamp.

Translation by Ming Di

Jade

Jade breathes with caution—
breathing in, into the worldly life, then out.
Self-contained, jade crosses a river.

I tried to stay calm last night like jade
with no thoughts or lust, forgetting my
seven orifices and nine openings,
my body flat, no ripples or wrinkles.
Eyes closed, I became a breath of air.

Translation by Ming Di

Questions of Cranes

Deep in the mountains, I've seen cranes
in the form of pillars. Or even of liquid, of gas,
or spring mud curled up at the roots of solemn azaleas,
their wings withdrawn.
I've seen the birds, the fictitious kind,
their pure white color full of rejections, but
growing into a more suitable form on doomsday.

For dying people, to raise cranes is a game,
like a minority religion. Writing poetry
is something else: the "crane"
in this line can be totally replaced. But
never ask what creatures cry for the cranes.
They cry to the east, which is to the west as well.
They cry for backroom politics, and for street revolutions.

Like tonight, in the roaring sound of the fan in my bathroom
I sit for a long time
as if I will never take a step from here.
I am a common man, having never raised a crane or killed one.
I know my suffering is ending, along with my duties.
I put on a pure white bathrobe, striding to the place
of a bystander, although in a former time
I was the one who made comments.

Translation by Ming Di

D O U   F E N G X I A O

Ferry

Just when I think about getting across
the river, a boat comes toward me.
"Wait for me," I say aloud.

It's an old vessel marked by the passing years,
blue-and-red stripes, and brown rust
glaring.

Has there been such a boat on the river?
No one has seen what it was before.
Nor will I see what it will be in the future.

At this moment, over the water
sheltered by the mountains' reflections,
the boat comes quietly. It comes as it is needed.

Is this what I've been waiting for? Has it imagined me
as well? If it comes from my mind,
why isn't it a new boat?

The river is immensely empty. A cloud moves
as if pulling a pennant flag. I stand by the riverside
watching the boat come straight to me like a sailor.

Translation by Ming Di

Paralyzed Miner, Ferry Interior,
Three Gorges Section, 2001.
Photograph by Linda Butler.

This man's legs were crushed in a mine
collapse, paralyzing him for life. After
months in a hospital, he was taken
back to his village where his wife and
three children awaited him. The min-
ing company gave him a $7,000 settle-
ment and a personalized blanket.

Three Poems

THINK OF THIS WORD

This thinking, full empty,
this meaning, the mine, the spellbound,
the force from the coal seam,
the blood seamed deep in the formation,
the intersection where humans are spilled out,
the shake of the left hand, the hole that's left there—
think of this death, this don't-know-how-to-die.

Inside the sand, upright spines are buried,
and on their shoulders are cemeteries and construction sites.
Inside the tent, death is too much exposed.
The burial releases a force.
Before that, invested in the pit is the credit of time.
From the center flow out the pre-death events,
in silence.
Above the constructed and to-be-constructed wilderness
is the history, in which no one
lives in a safety zone.
No watching, no motivation
to watch. But in watching it
we return to it, partially.

This—this plural form of promises in the wild weeds . . .

WHITE SAND GATE

Pool tables face the deformed statues, nobody—
Giant fishing nets hang on the broken walls, nobody—
Bicycles are locked to the pillars, nobody—
Three of the angels on the pillars are shot down, nobody—
The asphalt ocean water will soon rush in, nobody—
One horse is left on the beach, but nobody—
You stand there, and you become a surplus—nobody,
nobody would take what they see as home.

GRATITUDE

In returning what we've taken, we take again,
and we're grateful to the emptied space, our land.

We expand its geography to the mining zone
in the off-hours, and are grateful to its past, a wide land.

Our ancestors refuse to be plaster statues,
we're grateful to the trees—they stand in line as our families.

Tombstones will no longer measure the groundwater levels,
we're grateful to them, singers of the earth.

We bow to the earth that continues to give,
grateful to its deep messages that reach our knees.

When the blessings are not sure where to go,
we're grateful to the hidden journeys.

When the emptied space reveals the wheat field underneath,
we're grateful for the unexpressed apologies.

When the trees send a lyrical force to touch our shirts,
we're grateful to the stars that point down

to what we should be grateful to
but has been concealed from us . . .

Translations by Ming Di

NATALIE FENAROLI

Kansas

We used to think the world was flat,
no dips or craters,
like a land stretched to that endless line
crossing the horizon.
A desolate sky meets a dull earth,
as the heavens' finger drops from the blue void,
pressing to the ground
to pop the pimples of the landscape.
One barn gone,
a car swept away.
The sky roils,
its underbelly a writhing nest of nebulous snakes.
The earth shivers to the bone.
Emptiness clings to the soul of the sky.
Famished by an earthly hunger,
the sky licks the planet,
clearing the fields.
The sky moans in hunger,
whipping the grass in anger,
gnashing its teeth and howling to high hell,
gorging itself on the mire.
A freight train they say.
The sound of the angry monster sky
hell bent on
desecrating the face of the earth.
But no.
It is a beast with a will,
and a yearning,
to make that celestial sphere
flat as a Kansas cornmeal pancake.
Only cold skeleton-handed trees
reach upward as if to beg it
for mercy.

Twice Alive (excerpt) _____

mycobiont just beginning to en-
wrap photobiont each to become
something else its own life and a
contested mutuality twice alive
algal cells swaddled in clusters

you take a 3-lens jeweler's loupe to inspect the holdfast
of the umbilicate lichens then the rock tripe lichens
then the Amitaba Buddha mushroom, cambric in color,
swarming with a kind of mite that has no anus
then the delicious chanterelles called Trumpets of Death

I crush oak moss between finger and thumb
for its sweet perfume persistent on
your skin when I touch your throat so slow
to evaporate the memory of seeing
sunburst lichen on the sandstone cliff

but if herbivores eat wolf lichen they
die and if carnivores eat it they die
writhing in pain with the exception of mice
it is rarely possible to tell
if lichen is dead or alive

Two Poems

RAIN OR FISH

Suddenly lightning
flashes and the rain
is transformed into fish, each transparent blue
falling in a torrent
across the earth

Below,
some of the people are startled and panic,
they cower here and there and cover their heads.
Others are ecstatic and open
their welcoming arms.

I blink my eyes and cry aloud:
Look, the sky is having a dream.

Translation by Ming Di and Frank Stewart

Rain (yu) *and fish* (yu) *are homonyms in Chinese but have different tones.*

WATER BIRD

Something streaks across the sky
plunges into the water and rises
—was it merely the sky's shadow?

The bird paddles along,
slaps at the surface, then stops.
What shall I do? It hesitates as if
considering its options:
turn around, dive under, or fly away—
three possibilities to choose from,
three paths, three directions.

The bird turns back,
Then returns, and suddenly dives as if
overcoming some obstacle in its path.
It surfaces, and then rises into the air
in the direction of the horizon.
The bird is certain that it can have
all three choices, as if they were all one.

Only such a bird knows the meaning of freedom.
But it does not speak.

The bird has no need at all to speak of freedom.

Translation by Liang Yujing and Frank Stewart

Summer Night Wings _____

In the royal blue wash of July night
a yellow glow surrounds the lone street lamp,
whirling school of flying insects punch drunk

on bright light, dancing a frenzied foxtrot
in thick air, their wings whirring loud in amped-
up concerto. More love than you would think

existed in the world. But other love
waits in the wings, so to speak. A ballet
troupe in fur and leather enters the fray,

gliding through the crowd, a soundless dive.
Glorious bats, intoxicated with this trance
of love on the wing, this lavish wheeling dance.

Asia Bronze

Asia bronze Asia bronze
My grandfather died here my father died here I too will die here
You are the only place to bury people
Asian bronze Asian bronze
What likes to be suspicious and loves flying is a bird
What drowns everything is sea water
Yet your master is a blade of grass   living on its own small waist
And holding wildflowers—
Their palms and their little secret

Asia bronze Asia bronze
Have you seen those white pigeons? They are white shoes
Qu Yuan left on the beaches
Let us put the shoes on—yes we   along with the rivers
Asian bronze Asian bronze
We beat drums we beat hard and the heart that dances in the darkness
    we call it moon
And this moon   is primarily composed of you

Translation by Ming Di

Two Poems

SOME QUESTIONS

Who first asked it?
The sand or the footprint,
the remembering or the forgetting?

*

A house, a door, an hour—
which is frame, which picture?

*

Where found, old grief-joy,
your salvage-yard windows and shutters,
your emergency, your emergence?

*

Me, you / us, them—
what
molecule   cell   creature
came first to feel it?

*

Was it painful?

*

How came separation to chisel,
to cherish, to chafe?

*

Hammock of burning carbon
life wove from,
hammock life slept in,
unraveling—

did you find us useful,
interesting,
comic?

*

Will you miss them,
the cruelty and hunger,
the manatees and spoonbills,

awe's inexplicable swaying?

A BUCKET FORGETS ITS WATER

A bucket forgets its water,
its milk, its paint.
Washed out, reused, it can be washed again.

I admire the amnesia of buckets.

How they are forthright and infinite inside it,
simple of purpose,
how their single seam is as thin of rib as a donkey's.

A bucket, upside down,
is almost as useful as upright—
step stool, tool shelf, drum stand, small table for lunch.

A bucket receives and returns all it is given,
holds no grudges, fears,
or regret.

A bucket striking the mop sink rings clearest when empty.

But not one can bray.

HUANG BIN

Two Poems

WALKING IN THE WOODS

Walking in the woods in the summer, I see
trees flourishing in a complicated way.
Uplifting, they are positive, thriving, their interior
grows like human ambitions and swelling desires.
I think of the word 木 *mu*, simple and quiet,
born to be silent, born in the deep fall,
its first appearance stunning. Shocking.
木 *mu* of four seasons slows down to acquire a 木 image.
Look at its shape with branches and a trunk, created
in more than a few days, or a few weeks.
A simple beauty. A holistic miracle. A concrete abstract.
木 lives in the woods, in nature, in the human heart,
immortal in a mortal world.
木 becomes paper, and paper's full of the words 木.
How does 木 in words meet 木 in the woods? How?

Translation by Ming Di

ODE TO SHENNONGJIA FIRS

In the whiteness of early February, fog spreads
around the snow dictatorship of Shennongjia Mountains.
Along the shady streams are firs forty meters high,
each a green body, white beard and hair.
Each tree stands alone, far away from the others,
in its own coldness and solitude.
They like to look at each other
from a distance. They are tall and straight,
looking down, and looking over the others.
Their needles, thick and straight, look up in V-shape lines.
In June, male and female cones will blossom,
and mature in October. But sometimes they are shy
in showing their hearts. They wait two years to grow fruit.
What touches me most is how they die.
In Shennongjia Mountains, the firs live a hundred and
eighty years, then they begin to die—
first they wither from the top, then down and down in segments.
Within a few years, they've gone over their lives again,
from top to bottom.
When the dying reaches their roots, they fall intact
in a big roar. Each tree still holds its shape,
lying down all in one body.
Years later, they will still look like trees and this is the most
thorough death of a plant, perhaps. They possess
the art of dying.
Snow or wind will not wake them again.
If you step on one, you will feel like
you are losing your feet in mud—
their entire bodies have turned into earth,
into the living shape of firs.

Translation by Ming Di and Kerry Shawn Keys

Faster Than a Lightning Flash

The river courses like my blood.
It's aware of my thirst
when I'm on the road. Run.

I run away from the poverty.
The forest is becoming green again.
What else has moistened my shirt?

Run. The forest flies up
My heart quivers and shakes off its fatigue.
My life as short as a lightning flash—
before I have time to grieve
I'm pushed along. Run.

Translation by Ming Di

*Wanxian Old Town, Wanxian, 2001.
Photograph by Linda Butler.*

*When this photograph was taken,
some schools and neighborhoods
of old Wanxian were still intact;
the hospital (lower right) is being
dismantled. Sixty thousand people
were relocated, many receiving
only a fraction of the money
promised them.*

New Port, Wanxian, 2003.
Photograph by Linda Butler.

When the reservoir reached the shores of Wanxian in June 2003, there was still much work to do. Workmen were laying stone slabs to secure the landfill embankment and create a quay. Many of the remaining buildings would be torn down to prepare for a new business district at the wharf's edge.

Two Poems _____

ELECTRIC PSALM

May those deer wandering on the blue screen's green
woods find a stream there. May they remain safe
from whistling bullets till bullets become spent whirring
rounds. May kids from the concrete metropoli find those deer,
their gaze a tissue of fear fetched far from video camera
or computer chip till the laptop becomes sheer altar,
for blessed are those who see among circuitry and glare,
those who can tap a letter's key and know its curved
weight the way deer know the angle of trees and the earth's
curve, yet are fooled by a headlight's glare—or know downwind
an arrow's whoosh, and blessed those whose legs don't buckle,
who run till those woods skirt suburbia's pixeled dusk
toward which they gaze then turn back to a darkness
leaking more, a kind of noise or low flickering your eye
catches on the screen, not the snow falling through red
leaves, snow that builds, joining city to woods, but a restless
drone joining antennae to tree from which the animals turn
farther, todays toward tomorrow, unblessed their blessed darkness.

DEDICATION

To the alphabet texted through ten million iPhones
or shot through names of the living and dead.
To the letter X that lives between numbers.
To "I" that wants to become 1, and to "O" that lusts for the sun.
To the bees and their furious hexagons.
To the cubicles rising in a skyscraper not beyond
voices carrying a threat. To the echo of footsteps in a stadium.
To him to her to them. To all the screams and glass
splintering back toward windows. To those born
crying, awaiting their names. To the hungry,
shaking seconds out like salt. To the animals that are
numbered. To the churches and slaughterhouses
and to the words that multiply. To those
who push *Send*. To all knowledge finally swept
toward information then satellite
encoded. To *to,* how it keeps
marvelously opening, and to everyone's eyes
in the digital haze.

A Question to Ask Once the Honeymoon Is Over_____

Big around as my bike helmet and high as my ankle, the box turtle
was halfway from my side of the road
to the other. The warm sun felt delicious;
my legs, strong, and it was almost
to the center line. I hadn't been passed by a car
for miles. Figuring if it was still there, I'd pick it up
on the way back, I cycled past.

                                                 Years before,
the woman across the street was shaped like that turtle,
or more like a toadstool, really, squat bell
of a body atop the thin stalks of her legs, milky and bare
beneath her frayed black housedress. It hurt her to move—clear
even from my second-story window—so she brought
her trash out in increments, in small, bursting
grocery bags. She tossed each out the door onto the porch, then
nudged them, one step to the next, before easing—carefully,
painfully—herself down, a step at a time. Then she toed them,
finally, slowly, slowly into a crumpled heap at the curb. I left
my window to help; then took her trash out every week after.
                                           That story—
                   I hadn't yet
                             told it to my wife, had I?

                   But there was the turnaround
quicker than expected and I spun
to find a beat-down bus trailed by all the fuming cars
that hadn't passed me.
                        Steadying my handlebars against the wind,
I rode back hard, zigging around crushed
squirrels and tire-splayed birds.

                              The turtle
was just where I'd left it, but with the top of its shell
torn away. The dead turtle,
a raw red bowl, its blood slashing the twinned yellow lines
into an unequal sign,
                  as in a ≠ b, as in thinking about doing the right thing
is not the same as doing it. As in, how many times
did I watch that old woman shuffle bags down the stairs
(*really, how many?*) before I went from watching
to helping? As in, with my wife beside me
I am the woman who does not hesitate
to lay down her bike and give a small life
safe passage. As in, I biked slowly
home, told no one. As in:

            Will she love me
                      less when she learns
            I am not equal
                      to the person I am when she is watching?

The Shape of the Ocean

When you ask me what the ocean's shape is like
I should bring you two sacks full of sea water.
They are the ocean's shape, like two eyes,
or what the ocean seems like because of a pair of eyes.
You caress them, as though dabbing away
two scalding tears, and tears
are also the ocean's shape, their transparency
arising from identical souls.
Leaning the sacks together
does not make the oceans wider. From their freshness,
two not-fish are about to emerge.
You sprinkle water on the sand-like flour.
Bread is an ocean's shape.
Before you slice it with the blade of a sail
it is already going away, like a boat from a harbor. The plastic bags
lying flat on the table are an ocean's shape,
with their tides ebbing from the beaches.
When an actual tide ebbs,
the salt that remains is the ocean's shape.
You don't believe me? I should bring you a sack
of sea water and a sack of sand, which are the shapes of the ocean.
You say yes, then no; then not-yes,
not-no. Go and look at yourself,
you are also an ocean's shape, even though you say,
"I am only the shape of myself."

Translation by Ming Di and Frank Stewart

J I A N G   T A O

Snow in Ulan Bator

Monday morning I got up early, thinking I was home,
scrounged a drink of water in the bathroom,
turned my socks inside out and slipped them on
as if what happened last night was nothing.

But it's snowing outside. After only one night
the grassland retreats in haste,
exposing a great cluster of Japanese cars
sinking into bottomless mud. This

I'm actually already familiar with
It's been this way for more than a century, from Tokyo to Beijing,
and now again here.
Straight-nosed wide-mouthed commuters,

their faces exhausted from stuffing themselves
with potatoes cooked in the freezing wind,
are going to work now, shotguns on their shoulders
replaced by a forest of black umbrellas.

But I'm still in my underwear,
switching quickly between BBC and CNN.
The white-haired anchorman always looked arrogant,
but now he speaks proletarian English.

I'm skeptical, understanding half of what he says.
I guess that a great shift might come
—but not local mountains becoming golden hills
nor Pyongyang turning into Beijing.

I sense that what was looming
is coming, so I decide to get dressed, go downstairs
and join the crowded Far East poetry festival
and during my reading throw in some foreign words

like "Black Monday" and stuff like that,
implying: this good snow, isn't it just in time?

Translation by Tony Barnstone and Ming Di

Two Poems

MOUNTAIN SPRING

Old mother never went back to our hometown.
She often spoke to us as if in dream:
In this highland where the buckwheat grows,
a person misses bracing spring water.

No wonder she would sit alone at the window,
wondering from what place a bird had flown.
She would watch a cloud for a long time
until it disappeared where the wind blew.

No one can change life's background color:
A fireplace hisses under the tile roof
and courtyard roosters crow constantly.

In fact, a person can have simple needs
that are more difficult than touching sky.
She can't drink the heart-water of that spring.

HOMETOWN WIND

Mother often thinks of wind from home.
When this happens, she will sketch the wind.
No wonder in the epics of our tribe
eternal wind is planted in stone words.

Wind from the abysmal universe
passes through the void of wheat on earth.
Wind is the gate between our life and death.
Who can predict its future and direction?

Mother said, *If you can know the language
of wind, you'll know why our Yi people's flute
produces such naively cryptic sound.*

The wind still blows and I am a wind listener.
Today I start to get it, vaguely.
Wind is the only immortality.

Translations by Tony Barnstone and Ming Di

Call Her Suoma

Call her Suoma*
in the name of love we share
in the last, this, and next life.
Love her—love her breathtaking color
    from blooming,
the traces she left
in the wind the rain the scorching sun.
Nothing disdains her beauty: she is pure
like ice jade
but she is not just pretty and frail.
Her sonorous voice comes from the air,
the revolving stream, the soil.
Love her.
And embrace her barren body
like heaven and earth
and everything that grows on earth
with natural birth and death
in the world even though the world
doesn't care where the wind blows,
where you're from what you are or where you're going.
She has her own garden, her old dream
and her clearly sounding name—
Call her Suoma out loud
like calling yourself.

Translation by Ming Di

* *Yi name of azalea
flower; also the most
common name for
women in the Yi
region.*

Boy and Dog, Wanxian, 2001.
Photograph by Linda Butler.

In this communal dwelling, a court-
yard provided space for prosperous
residents to keep pets and socialize.
Six months after this photograph was
taken, the dwelling was gone; the fam-
ilies had moved to a high-rise, unable
to take their dogs because the new
apartments were too small for them.

A Sacred Mango

We gathered in front of our City Hall
exploding firecrackers and beating drums and gongs.
Thousands of people came over
to receive a gift for our city from Chairman Mao.
It was a golden mango carried by a big truck
accompanied by three other trucks,
all of which were planted with colorful flags
and loaded with golden chrysanthemums.

The mango was exhibited in the center of the hall.
We lined up to look at it
and to show our gratitude and respect.

But that night
some curious child tasted the fruit
and was not caught.
Our mayor, frightened and outraged, said,
"Damn it, if I knew which son of a rabbit bit the mango
I would turn his whole family
into counter-revolutionaries!"

But what could we do?
We substituted a wooden mango for a real one.

Salt

I was trying to remember
what reminded me of the gulls

we saw mired on the shore of
Salt Lake, as if blown or trampled

into the muck, unable to struggle
free again, beaks muddy, wings coated,

flapping and flapping, heat-dazed,
paralyzed, and all the time, salt

doing what salt does, dessicating skin,
mummifying the tender flesh.

How the bones of a half-buried wing
jutted from sand, beseeching.

I cannot even save myself.

LEI PINGYANG

Happy Ants

In their dreams, they do running drills.
First, over a field. Then, over the
night. For a while they can't see
anything. Some of them are beaten
by the grass, their ribs broken.
In the end, they start to run around the city
in circles. A tiny, little army
that you can neglect. They are being drilled
in their own dreams.

Translation by Ming Di

Three Poems

AUTUMN IN AN ALMOST-NO-TOWN

There are eleven shapes of autumn
moving in the wind from south to north
exchanging forty names. Palm trees,
sycamore trees, and poplar trees
speak at the same time of the same cloudy, dark
sky. Clouds hang, and descend like waterfalls.
They want to return somewhere. The river?
All of a sudden, the sky starts to circle
like a bamboo sieve sifting grains from the sunshine
above. The pedestrians walk slowly,
forever hungry, forever looking upward.

IN A QUARRY

Every day I dream the same dreams,
passing through a quarry at midnight.
Stones burst open, cut, ground,
carried away along a thin cable in midair.
Anguish comes from the interior
of the stones, the indivisible core of darkness.
Everything wears down
when shared, but not pain.
It comes freely like the fall
of a solid stone, painful but pure.

A PENINSULA FACING THE EAST

When rocks expand like vegetation,
eastward, eastward,
tourists get less crowded here.

You draw in the wind an outline of a peninsula,
fold it—an increasingly clear rim
of twilight.

You walk into the center of the twilight. It
moves with you eastward, in a shimmering,
dimming gleam like a candlelight.

I open and spread you, the in-the-wind entity,
a faint blue thing,
and extend it to a dark-green bay.

From four to seven p.m., I repeatedly fold, open,
shaped and unshaped.

Translations by Ming Di

Temple Stairs, Shibaozhai, 2000.
Photograph by Linda Butler.

These 500-year-old stone steps descend
from a mountainside temple. China's
Bureau of Culture Protection planned
to build a wall to protect the temple
from the rising waters. A sign (upper
right) indicates the height the reservoir
was expected to reach in 2009.

LI HONGWEI

Dreaming of a Tiger's Corpse

Those who dream of tigers on a rainy day
possess an ancient forest inside their bodies
where there are hundreds of green, lush trees and calm birds.
Sun rays are packed, unable to find a way to flow out.
Even if they poke through the leaves and pour to the ground,
there will be only colorful tapestry stitches.

The father of the public beasts rises.
He walks at ease, eyes far-seeing.
He doesn't carry weapons, just his flashing teeth.
With his howling, he patrols the vast dream
and with a real tail, left and right,
mopping the fern grass and earth, sweeping the wind.
He leaps up to the crouching boulder, and
with one big bite eats up the rain and the dreamers.

It's on a raining day like this,
I dream of a tiger's corpse.
Ragged, it's halfway immersed in a paddy field,
two hind legs completely gone.
Luckily, its mouth and wiring are intact.
With electricity, it can smile a tiger smile
and sing soaking-wet songs.

Translation by Ming Di and Kerry Shawn Keys

Look What I Have

I have anger that looks decent as black satin.
I have patience that drips like water through stones.
I have the hesitancy of a kind person
when he or she occasionally lies.
I have sadness and its twin daughters:
one is called sorrowful and the other softhearted.
I have the appearance of the poor,
gestures of the rich.
I have the quietness of a woman knitting a sweater,
and wildness as when she stays in a farmhouse overnight.
I pass under a suspension bridge
where a clown is staging a performance.
Look, death has seized me but I go my usual way,
tasting a new wine while laughing.
I have the temperament of a fool who's also lazy.
I live in the field under an old eucalyptus tree.
I have a singing voice deep and winding—
no one dares take it, or anything
from me.

Translation by Ming Di and Frank Stewart

Two Poems

ORANGE IN THE WILDERNESS

sun rises in Southeast
orange in wilderness
yellow in orange
sunshine in orange
shadow in orange
orange next to orange
orange on the roof

sun sets in West
orange in wilderness
sun sets in orange
gray in orange
moon in the eaves
night without orange

Translation by Ming Di

Arrival

I have reached autumn. I am done with talking.
Now, the pear tree decides, Let all the pears fall.
Then, the pear tree also decides, Let all leaves fall.
I wait for a decision, an echo—
From the south to the north: summer's loud curtain fall.
But I only faintly hear pear flowers calling to the pears
and the pears calling to the pear flowers.

The Pear Tree and the Pear

I hear, beyond the horizon.
Deep autumn, day opens, night winds in the valley quicken the
    egg-stones,
Robert Frost's ladder's sticking through the pear tree,
high into the pear leaves.
Frost is not here—only a horse saddle is here.
I am not here—only a bamboo basket is here.
A pear asks another pear—all pears ask pears,
Why are our pear pits all sour, a sourness stretching to antiquity
    and back?
A pear replies, This is not a pear's decision. It is the tree's.
A pear tree suddenly shivers.
A tree says, Maybe it is the white flower of spring.
Another tree says, Maybe it is the greening wind, the moistening rain,
    or the shadowing light.
Another one says, Maybe it was that ladder. Those chairs.
The sun crosses noon. You don't hear the babbling pears.
Sundown past the mountain ridge. You don't see the yellowing pears.

Translations by Tony Barnstone and Denise Wong Velasco

Two Poems

GOD COMES TO A SMALL BUS STATION

Three or five cottages,
        one or two lights.
Here I am, as small as an ant, nowhere in the middle
of the grand Hulunbuir Grassland, having to spend a night
        at a nameless station
alone, bearing the cold loneliness but feeling peaceful.

Behind me stands the tiger of a cold winter night.
Behind that is a clear open road.
Behind the road is the Ergun River flowing slowly,
        a shimmering light in the darkness.
Behind that is the endless birch forest,
        the wilderness of wildernesses.
Behind that are quiet stars low in the sky,
        a blue velvet of soft curtain.

And behind that is the vast North where God resides.

A SMALL TOWN IN SOUTHERN JIANGSU

Between the metropolises lies a little kingdom
of singing birds and streaming creeks.
Yellow rapeseeds, the primary residents,
are flowering in this season. A dragonfly and a butterfly
are the permanent King and Queen.
Deep tranquility is the keynote, so ancient
You can hear crickets quiver in the wind.
Very few cars or horse carriages pass by.
But something is happening in the slow zone between the fields
and hillside, a historical moment so tragic and so early
in the morning. Look at the grass and trees, their heads chopped off.
I'm shocked. The forever peacefulness broken.
The smell of dying vegetation is strong, and everlasting.
This most violent and darkest hour in the history
of plants will be described lightly as "trimming."

Translations by Ming Di and Kerry Shawn Keys

Two Poems

CASTOR

I remember a plant with leaves
palm on outstretched palm
nine-fingered each
long I thought, without remembering its name
before I was decapitated
I shouted out
castor   castor

I remember he said something
about wanting to burrow
from my vagina to my womb
so that I'd be pregnant with him
give birth to him
so that I'd love him
as with a child
unconditionally and always
I remember saying nothing
a buzzing noise came from my mouth
like seeds being chewed to bits
castor   castor

WEDNESDAY'S SHIP OF PEARLS

When autumn enters the constant hour
I begin to crush and grind
out the recipe for knowledge
not bitter enough, I think
these viscous memories chewed once
in a while should suffice
my silences   I have to

swallow a fishbone, soundless
I have to stomach
that bit of rusted iron
I think it best this life
be spent on web-spinning
drawing endless radians on a bridge
so as to form that geometry
called fortune
on a Wednesday, I will see
a ship arrive, brimful of pearls

Translations by Ming Di

Saving

Even with drought, with gray greasy
water the wild grass grows,
shallow roots trolling in veiny
networks, to sprout yellow-
baby patches, and all in one
morning burst monstrous
straw filaments robust
as bushes in a rainy
fallow year. Even goats may
not eat it, that gnaw on cacti thorn,
lip tires in abandoned canyons.
True trees need deep watering,
and there is none to be had today
when sunshine is a curse
and stark skies blush for nothing
at dusk and dawn. Shamelessness undoes
us—spigots flowing, saving
gray water for roots that alone
can trawl these withered earths.

Three Poems

A POTTED PLANT

Those things that have nothing to do with the heart—
are no better than a potted plant

Those that have something to do with the heart—
are no better than a tree

Tree is God
mother
hometown
an abbreviation of these words

I pass by a tree in a village
I ask it—"Do you have God?"

It says: "What is God?"
"A widower who loses things endlessly"
"Like me"
"Like me, howling in a low, dry voice"

It smiles, a bitter smile
then we turn silent

MAY

Green lions are climbing mountains
numerous green lions are climbing mountains
newly born
with bushy manes

They are determined to sit quietly in the mountains
practice meditation and maybe become vegetarians too

Wildness untamed
they want to race with springtime
to see who can run faster from one peak to another

"Wait for me! I am wearing pink
and it's slowing me down"

THE PACIFIC OCEAN

we are in the process of losing. in the ocean. carrying all the things
we have lost. flowing to the east. to the other shore
of glamor

feelings. beliefs. memories. drifting farther and farther away—

that's when our tears will pour like rain. insignificant
they will flow into the mighty ocean. then we'll turn around. someday
we will turn around. to welcome what flows from another place—

feelings. beliefs. memories. and we will feel an
excitement. our blood will surge anew. and we'll be astonished by
the secretly replaced moment. how. that moment.
is forgotten by time

by then
I will have a son
you will be. on my breast
sucking

Translations by Michelle Yeh

Night at Ocean Corner, and Women

Ocean Corner, Ocean Corner,
a fishing village
in the shape of a fisherman's footprint,
immerses in water like a fan spreading its spikes.
A black shirt with sparkling stars
blows across
when night falls. And here

people go to sleep early, with salty air outside
the windows. Nearby, evening lights
on fishing boats scatter, a sign of
nets down in the ocean—they've waited
a thousand years for the fish.
Night is dark. Children cry as if there're no parents
around—they're in deep dreams.
Children cry. But it's time

to go to sleep. Children get quiet. So do the small hours
of deep night at Ocean Corner. Everyone sinks into
happiness with a bubbling smile
and this is the most beautiful moment—
no voices by the men's side gently pushing:
"Time to go to sea."

Translation by Ming Di

Rehearsal for Ending

Feathers—
or birds, or leaves

fell slowly into the snow
among the dark thin hounds

and their hunters,
obscuring the wet bark torsos

of the trees,
larger

even than the black-clad
skaters on celadon

ponds, grim as the
morning sky

and melting as,
seconds later,

snow—I'm sure—was floating up—
flakes or white feathers

losing their scant
gravity

as the ice began to burn
along the edges

and the drifts of tulle
veiling the long grass—

already slowed, elongated—
tangled in muddy clouds of web

as Mahler appeared—
I think it was Mahler

—or something had happened to the air,

echoing the distance among those same
increasing shades of green, in notes

or in something that trembles—

something else, something far apart

as the roiling gray of a fishtail-
braided cloud, years

and seconds later

in that pentimento of rain,
grainy and dark

and darkening the distances of green
waters and murky fields

until it seems barely possible to make out
the few abandoned fishing boats

and almost impossible to tell
whether the two tall stalks

are cut-off sails
or the edges of self-pruning cottonwoods

that have grown, in confusing weathers,
up through salt

and through the teal and emerald of
the slippery reeds of shore toward the roiling gray corn

of the clouds in their horizontal twisting above shards of wall
below. And then white moths,

like motes, floating into the star-dark sky,
just as after the box is opened and things fly out

some of them are still alive, and light,
even as the sail-cloak darkens over the body

and the lover extends the fingers again toward the wound, and tries,
and cannot stand.

Gallina Canyon

All night the cattle bellowed,
cows and calves of the separated herd
seeking each other under helpless stars,
never sleeping, even when the dog slept.

Cows and calves of the separated herd,
loud as the far-flung buffalo
never sleeping, even when the dog slept.
I heard a world of other animals,

loud as the far-flung buffalo,
loud as mother bears calling to their young.
I heard a world of other animals
filling the canyon with their awful song.

Loud as mother bears calling to their young,
a night of wailing from the walls,
filling the canyon with their awful song
from open lungs among the cottonwoods.

A night of wailing from the walls.
I could not sleep. The night was at a loss.
From open lungs among the cottonwoods,
mothers were calling to their young.

I could not sleep. The night was at a loss.
All night the cattle bellowed.
Mothers were calling to their young,
seeking each other under helpless stars.

MO FEI

Some Floating Time in Light—For You _____

Some days floating in light for you, some water for the trees,
some gentle wind for the new moon. Some whispering for the words,

the rest are evening lights for the clouds and the fairies.
Some plums for the twigs and branches, some rivers

for the wells. Some jade for the roofs and eaves.
Some windows for the walls, some walls for the ears.

Some beans around the house back and front, some rain
for the season. Some labor for those who don't work,

some ladders up and down for toon leaves and persimmons.
Some cats calling, some trespassing in the spring for a next life.

Some pains for growing, some pains for blooming.
Some birds for the evenings, and some evenings for the songs.

Translation by Ming Di

Two Poems _____

THE ZOO

I find a directory of paradise
and following the address compiled in the language of cannibals
I find a heavily guarded zoo
Calling me, a leopard moans,
"The cat burgled my food"
I caress the beast's fur
Pointing at the faraway morning star
the beast murmurs, "Don't provoke the goat
His horns are stilettos"
A sleepless golden fish misses the shark who covets her
Furious, the golden oriole
wants to duel the ants that molested her

I squat next to the hippo's yawn
thinking of man's belly tastes
Sticking out his chest, the praying mantis says from on high,
"I'll fight those humans to the end"
The panda heaves a deep sigh, "Aaa!
I've fought revolutionary struggle for tens of thousands of years,
    but my fur remains unchanged"
The tiger spots a typo in the Bible
and swears that Heaven is Hell

The hedgehog disagrees and says, "The clouds would like to wear silver"
I stop a pig couple sweetly in love
and tell them the ballet theater has been torn to ruins
The gander kills itself, its blood tainting the swan lake
When her periods dry up, the mosquito will turn in panic to any doctor,
and flagrantly flirt with the elephant
and eat corn on the cob, while the fox,
twisting around with a mysterious look, says,
"Did you know
I was the beauty queen Wang Zhaojun in my last life?"

The duck, a veteran informer,
earnestly reports, "The ostrich is an arms dealer
who lays nothing but A-bombs, getting countless orders"
The penumbra of the east proclaims, "Dawn"
I eventually realize that
the ostrich has become the ruler of paradise
who with tightly closed eyes shakes out feathers
and won't answer any of my questions
but sheds a plan for the Third World War
written in the language of birds in the sky

MY WHOLE LIFE

Just tangled intimately with a dove in the heavens for a while
Got mocked by the rainbow
Just sat Zen with pine trees on the cliff for a while
Got mocked by the moon
Just nestled up with the white sail in the waves for a while
Got mocked by the sea
Just got tipsy drinking with cranes in the woods for a while
Got mocked by the mushrooms

Just flowered with night-blooming cactus on the roadside for a while
Got mocked by white clouds
Just tumbled with autumn leaves for a while
Got mocked by the earth
Just dozed off in the arms of a lion for a while
Got mocked by the hunter
Peeped at the blackness of humanity just once
Got mocked by the gods

The rainbow imagines the moon's face
The sea imagines the mushrooms' breathing
And the white clouds: how they wish to float on the earth

Murdering hunters dream of being pardoned by guardian gods
Living a chaotic life like this
I scorn destiny

Translations by Tony Barnstone, Wang Hao, and Du Xian

Pasture

I will never be put out to pasture.
My old horses are put out to pasture,
some old horses are sold for dog food,
I feed dogs, share my food with them.
I might be meat for grizzlies if I stumble
into a nest of cubs. I have some memory
of seamen starving in a dory, drawing lots,
the loser: human steaks.
I will never be put out to pasture
long as *I* have something to say about it.
When I feed my opera-loving donkeys,
they bray: *We prefer you stay inside our fence.*
I live in the country, that compared
to the city, where I lived as a child,
is "out to pasture." Some have drunk
to others only with their eyes.
I drink and graze on Irish daisies that grow
in the countryside, and steel-girdled
cemented cities with my eyes. I want
all things in nature to ride my back.
The oceans are lighter than mountains,
I don't rear up, buck them off,
I am happy with my burden. Old horse,
I do not want to die fallen in a stall,
it's better outside, unhitched, reins dangling,
trying to get up on my own four legs.

Now I am just a man, not a metaphor.
I say to myself: *Here I am.*
I see a ram, horns caught in a thicket—
I free the ram, my hands bleed from thorns.
I do not believe sacrifice is a good cause.
I make a fire that warms me, it's not a burnt offering,
I have no favorite son.
I will not lay a hand on anyone,
except to comfort her or him.
I am grateful I can rest a while
in the kindness of green and rocky pastures.

An Embroidery Needle Made from a Water-Deer Fang

That embroidery needle made from
A water-deer fang—
Is it still fastened to the folded
Scarf in your hair?
Even with my dreams keeping watch,
Even in my soul's distress.

The sky has darkened, Mother,
The golden-feathered rooster
Is hanging on the lintel upside-down.
There on the threshold
That deer-fang needle
Guides the white-silver thread,
Waiting for my soul
To return to your embrace.

The sun has risen, Mother,
Open the carved wooden bowl.
The end of the water-deer needle
Is already pointing to your warm breath.
And at this moment, light shows itself
Throughout the stone-slab house.
Ah, that egg used to call back a wandering soul.
You eat the yolk, and I'll just eat the white.

The embroidery needle made from a water-deer fang—
Is it still in the felt pocket on your breast?
Can you still neatly embroider my soul
When you face the hills so lonely for so long?

Translation by Alexandra Draggeim

Joy

How trustworthy this ancient flame,
these potatoes with fresh mud, these cabbages,
the steam from the hot bread,
the frost on the radishes.

Now, I'm no longer a stranger
to myself,
nor is life elsewhere.

I'm tasting what the Buddhist Scripture says: joy.

The sunflower on my apron twists my body like love.
How are you, my old sun?

As good as you were in the Agrarian Age?
These wisps of smoke came from whose eyes?

I don't like the brisk new age, sun.
And this room keeping pace with the world . . .

A gusting echo in the morning dew and my sweat—I love
my old kitchen that smelled like a farm
with an empty bottle at dusk—I love

the me that sat still on a small stool.

Translation by Ming Di

Two Poems

GRAY ROAD NORTH TO SHENZHEN

Stretching, stretching.
Sober pavement, factories, a fog of skyscrapers,
looming gray clouds. Not one moving human
visible outside. How loud the loneliness of workers
abandoning villages for the long shifts,
brief breaks, stark apartments
where their second pair of gray pants waits.

ON THE OLD BACK CANAL ROAD BY THE
INTERNATIONAL HOTEL, GUANGZHOU

She is here
She is always here
Invisible makes her more here
Thunderstruck
Wondrous
Inside her I was so delicately constructed
Now she resides in me
Around me
We live together
Where the old water weaves between brick channels
Stacked lives
Laundry strung from balconies
Tiny geraniums popping red yeses
Somewhere a radio playing a very old song
Now sung by the air

The Fallacy of Snow

For a long time, people have ignored
the many fallacies of snow.
Now it's my turn to say something.

In the north, snow is grey
bearing nothing of purity.
Especially in the city, snow is pollution
twined with dust and
decaying to muddy water, which rots the city
in every street and
street corner.

A simple fact like this
no one wants to face, no one for a long time.
Is it because truth is lazy
or fallacy wears a beautiful coat?

Translation by Ming Di, edited by Tony Barnstone

ALAN MICHAEL PARKER

In the Next Life, a Tree

So I shall put on my tree hat
and my tree shirt and tree pants
and my root boots
and let my gouges show

and walk until I stay
and keep for the birds a home

and every so often
every so
I shall turn a little
to the light to grow

and I shall wrap
I wrap up in wind
so I can listen
to each inclination

jealous of lightning
blind in the snow
I shall let my colors decide

the years I will wear
all of my rings

and so many arms shall I have
and never need more
to carry
to carry the sky

An American Tale_____

Those men heaved garbage bags onto the pyres
until the air grew thick with melting plastic
and burned meat.
                              Months earlier, they'd gassed
the addled raccoons
where they crouched in the sewers
                                        until yellow haze
seeped from the manhole covers
into the street.
                        Later, door to door with pistols,
they found each listless cat
and put it down,
                        and trucked them all to the pyres,
where they scorched the pestilence
from their fur.
                        So tonight they were burning dogs—

*

A biological parasite
                                might move among a population,
surviving in one host only long enough
to pass itself on to other hosts.
                                        Increasingly,
scholars in the vanished Republic
                                        saw cultural ideas
as a kind of virus. Violence, terror, fascism
incubate inside a host mind
                                that passes them on to other
susceptible minds.
                        Sometimes, the host dies,
but his idea spreads among us.

*

Each black garbage bag

      sizzled on the flames,

then contracted suddenly

      so I could approximate the number,

of dead dogs it contained

      before the fire burned them away.

*

That the dogs were infected

      was an idea we got

from a report about a young girl who,
bitten in an alley,

      behaved queerly that evening,

eventually growing listless, feverish,
and, we heard,

    soon died.

The idea spread among us—

*

In the old days of the Republic,
I had a friend I called Charles
because I couldn't pronounce the name
his parents gave him.

Charles was a quiet boy,
fond of a neighborhood dog

        he'd taught to sit,

roll over, play dead.

     When his family vanished,

I'd watch that dog from my bedroom window
as it picked scraps from the neighbor's garbage.
Eventually, it, too,

    disappeared.

*

The idea was to keep some people from polluting
our country.

    The idea was they had a criminal

mentality,

    an incurable affinity for violence—

thievery, rape—that we could not tolerate
in our communities.

    (Charles' mother

on the front porch, sorting the day's mail
as sunlight speckled the gravel driveway;

Charles' father carrying groceries from the car
up the rain-flecked front steps.)

*

Of course,
                    we could not keep a virus
from entering the Republic,
                                        but we could slow it
where we saw it, in our collective
                                        awareness of dangerous ideas—
and so, when Charles vanished,
I sometimes fed his dog,
                              until the scraps
grew so few
                    no one could afford to feed any dogs.

*

Charles standing in his driveway
one snow-addled evening
                              holding out a cracker
until the dog finally lowered himself to the ground
and rolled quickly,
                    obediently,
                              onto his back.

*

The removal of some
                    who lived among us
facilitated the well-being
                              of those who deserved to stay,
or so I've been told. It has been decades,
and still I miss my friend,
                              whose absence
ensured the survival of the idea
of what it meant to be a citizen
                                        of the vanished Republic—

*

Their shapes stood out
                    in the tightening plastic
before the clarifying flames
                              made ash of them.

Village Destruction, Xiang Xi, 2001.
Photograph by Linda Butler.

The coal town of Xiang Xi was on a
cliff at the western entrance of Xiling
Gorge. Like many others, the town was
flattened. Because of the region's pov-
erty, hand tools rather than bulldozers
were used. Bricks, floor slabs, and
metal rebar were recycled.

QIU HUADONG

Two Poems

COLD VIEW

I walk to the wilds
All emotion is instantly frozen
Five flickering crows
Suddenly flash in my eyes
I am now lost
At a loss

Better I turn around and go
back, walk back,
from the crows, away
from the vastness over earthen tombs

PLANTING

I want to root roses in your shoes
sprout violets from your ears

I am running through a sky of big snow
Snow drops on my body, light as daylight

From pieces I piece together your gentle words
at times worrying at strange calligraphy

My words burst into your phrases and lines
My midnight blurs into your hair

I plant violets in your shoes
and roses sprout from your lips

Translations by Tony Barnstone and Henry Zhang

SUZANNE ROBERTS

Apocalypse at the Safeway

The first intercom announcement
is that they no longer take money.
Your dollars, they say, *are useless.*
The looting begins. Everyone rushes
the aisles, stealing Guatemalan coffee,
Puerto Rican rum, Chilean sea bass, French
wine. Another announcement: *No more*
produce will ever be delivered—you must learn
to eat only what you can grow. Outside,
January snows cover granite.

Meanwhile, a frenzy in produce—
I fill my pockets with Brazilian tangerines,
Mexican radishes, Ecuadorian asparagus.
A man with a shirtful of broccoli florets
shoves me out of his way. Rounds of iceberg,
scallions, and parsley fly through the air.
Pumpkins and pineapples are weaponry.
I leave produce, head for canned goods.

I fight an old woman for the last can of tuna.
For my cats! she cries, prying my fingers
from the can. Another woman runs past
with an armful of fancy canned peaches.
She stumbles, falls to her knees, cans wobble
silver in the murky darkness like suffocating fish.
The fluorescent lights dim, then flicker,
like theater lobby lights, indicating
the end of the intermission.

To Burn a World

We could be the world to each
                    other. We could
be light
        unfiltered by the evergreen,
the slow-burnt brown of both.
                    The warmth of our
multiplying bodies trapped between
                the layers
wrapped around the mountains,
                insulating
the sky.
    We could plant
                warheads
                and smokestacks.

There are several ways to burn
                    a world.
The friction between
                our neighboring hearts
intense enough to make
                    us spark and flame.
Grow clouds that the sky
            wouldn't grow itself.
Our bodies sticky,
            sheets of sweat building
in space behind knees
                when we stand too close
to the fire catching.

            We can watch it melt,
layers of paint sliding
                down the walls
like frosting on cake,

                    left out in the sun
when the birthday boy
                    realizes he hates
chocolate.
          Drywall and plaster curling
and peeling
            from wood beams that in turn will
buckle and wither.
               Brick and mortar turn
mercury, pool
          into rivers
                    on fire.

Downtown
          skid row
                    and everyone we know
will kiss each other
                    with blue-flame lips

Our friends and the scientists
                              will run tests
to know the source of
                    such heat, but they, too,
will start to feel faint. Papers,
                              computers,
their skin and their bones,
                         turn to lava and ash,
erasing everything,
          before we could explain.

NICHOLAS SAMARAS

Glossolalia of Wind

Yes, it spoke. Yes,
it had a color to it.
The wind was streaked with salt and language.

And gold light welled, the stone meadows
brimmed with it.
The hard tufts of green murmured

their testimonies, their martyrdom.
I spoke the lifespan of air.
I said after all had been said.

You come to every cave.
You put your hand on the skin of meaning,
the lifeline and the witness.

You take this.

Carpenter's House, Beishi, 2001.
Photograph by Linda Butler.

This carpenter constructed his own home in 1982 on a hillside overlooking the Yangtze. He designed the house, poured his own concrete bricks, and made the furniture by hand. He also raised bees to pollinate his tangerine trees. He was heartbroken to see the house destroyed.

Carpenter's House in Ruins, Beishi, 2003.
Photograph by Linda Butler.

When the carpenter returned to the
ruins of his house, only a ceramic water
vessel remained intact (middle right).
The sign "175-M" on the hillside predicts
the reservoir level in 2009. Six months
later, the land was under fifteen feet of
water and the carpenter had begun con-
structing a new home half a mile away.

Three Poems

CHESSBOARD

Flying back to Beijing
I look out—
a thin layer of whiteness
over the city. Snow.
A chessboard.
But who is playing chess
with me? Nobody, only me
and the bloody setting sun—
watching each other
across the snowboard.

Translation by Ming Di

CARPENTER

The carpenter,
stripped to his waist,
is striving to shape a block of wood
with his hand plane.
Shavings
surge up like sprays,
curly and soft,
giving off the scent of wood.
Swimming among wood,
he stretches out his arms
and draws them back.

A TAOIST PRIEST ON MOUNT KONGTONG

With great effort,
I climbed to the mountaintop.
There was a Taoist temple,
named Palace of the Jade Emperor.
At its front door
sat an old Taoist priest
striking the chime stone
for the pilgrims.
With a mallet in his left hand
for hitting the stone,
he held an apple in his right hand.
He struck the stone,
then gave his apple a bite,
struck again,
then bit again.
When hitting the stone,
he looked listless.
When he bit the apple,
his eyes shone.

Translations by Liang Yujing

SHEN WEI

Children of the Moon

Each time you return from the moon,
you whisper to me:
"I've been only to the garden nearby
for a little while—
a small insect there is dying…"
Phantasy and fantasy—
as if were the same and could both
escape from this world. But you, being lighter
than a cloud, can wander far
while I am imprisoned here even by the air,
rooted in this world by fate.
Each time you come back in the night dew,
you must have just arrived from the moon.
You don't mention our withering flowers
or the foul wind.
It's late fall, and I see something in your eyes
Making them bluer. Evening chill takes you by the skirt.
You already seem far away—but even when you are most distant,
when the moon and osmanthus trees will have died,
the scent from your lips will stay.

Translation by Ming Di

Pangolin Scales

You
wrote, Miss
Moore, about how
the pangolin, streaming
at high night from its stone-
lipped burrow, trespassing on Belgian
Congo moonlight, gibbous as a bell curve
from its paginated tail to its
gummed tongue, prolonged
for trickling down ant-
slickened trunk
crevices,
would

swirl
headlong down
the impenetrable drain it
makes of itself (Malay *pengguling*:
up-rolling thing), an involute, inexplicable
globe, plate lapping overlapping scalloped plate.
Only now, Miss Moore, I hate to report, it's plucked
like a junglesop fruit with its prehensile stem,
and handed off to traffickers, who parade it
into some high-rolling private dining
room in Guangdong or in Ho Chi
Minh City where its throat's
scis-

sored
steaming at the
upscale table as ardent
proof of freshness and gratitude to
the client whose *ummm!* stimulates the ritual
consummation of the business deal. "Considered
a delicacy," an anthropologically delicate phrase you'd
have relished, Miss Moore. But why? *Nostalgie de
la boue*? More a nostalgia to be bush-meat
eaters minus the mud in the Wild
West of Southeast China where
businessmen would
be men.

From
the black tricorner
of my notebook ajar, these
armored stanzas gleam expectantly.
Yes, Miss Moore, there's more. Olive, tan,
golden brown toenail scales, skinned or worked off
living pangolins one by one like artichoke leaves, scales
soft at first and milk white on the besotted nursling
riding its mammal's tail like a bath toy, ton
upon ton from Malaysia, Indonesia,
Zimbabwe, in luggage, under
timber, sacks of red beans,
bound

for West
Berkeley Wellness, say,
in the mild west of the East Bay
on 7th street, away from traffic, where
maternal practitioners of Traditional Chinese
Medicine, codified by Chairman Mao in the 1950s,
invite us over from their homepage window,
while visitors positively Yelp, and (now
unsearchable) pangolin scales, cool
and salty as the Pacific, are
administered to promote
menstrual flow and
lactation.

Small Notes in My Old Age

I return to the village and see lots of red peppers
sunbathing on the threshing floor with me,
giving warmth to the summer.
I put my hands to my eyebrow to make an arbor
as if installing an air conditioner in front of my eyes.
In fact, my forehead and my neck are making salt.
Lots of salt. Look, we've made this summer so salty!
And I'm not hospitable enough to myself, otherwise
why should I bring myself this full cup of liquor?
Yes, because I've finally had half of it.
As an antique holistic idealist, I demand everything be complete
including remnants of clouds, embers, and death.
However, I can accept what's second best: no old age.
Too many people give up the rest of their lives to be a martyr.
One life is too short to accommodate, might as well leave.
I am so extreme. I either fly up to eat people, or dive
into the sea to watch the stars—the sky collapses,
sea water overflowing. If my old age coincides with this earth,
why aren't we doomed on the same day? If the earth can't wait
for my urgent but sweet deadline, I will say to the world:
Come sooner!

Translation by Ming Di and Kerry Shawn Keys

South Gate, Dachang, 2001.
Photograph by Linda Butler.

The town of Dachang was a perilous,
four-hour boat ride up the Daning
River tributary. The villagers believe
that the gate is more than 1,700 years
old. The painted line on the left indi-
cates how high the reservoir was
predicted to rise in 2009.

What We Used to Call a River

There used to be clouds then
and the sky was blue
and from either the twelfth floor over the water
or the back porch near the redbud
we used to admire them both
and it could have been red—the sky—may god forbid
but what it was, at least to human eyes—
who knows the physics knows this—
the sky was blue because of the radiation,
shorter wavelengths and such,
and you would have loved it—you who watched
Body and Soul with John Garfield
and *The Wild Ones*, with Clark Gable and Marilyn Monroe
and you would have played with the clouds
alligators that ate their prey, lovers who
bumped their foreheads before the transformation
the wind alone starting the quarrel,
sitting by what we used to call a river.

Two Poems

BLAND LIFE, BLUNT POETRY

Apples change genes, oranges change genders,
words become absolutely tyrannical under the shadow of -ism.
I speak but say nothing; you oppose and oppose everything.
The paradox of rhetoric leads me to the way of poetry,
I travel valleys and gullies like a huge bird in the sky, only to see
fruits become symbols. Too symbolic,
the toughness of apples, the brutality of oranges. To find gentleness
I have to clear away other words from the pile. I plane off
the snobby and sneaky ones, they've been trying to use the old against . . .
Or let me put it another way, they act as if they were authorities,
as if they were ministers, or even emperors, of words.
The kingdom of language is decadent. How have I tolerated it
for so long? I'd rather see chaos. I say
chaos is good! When apples fly in the air
oranges become shields against the -ism. Or when I see
apples swimming in the ocean of words like mermaids,
oranges a pack of camels carrying feelings on their backs, I feel
liberated. I feel so liberated I start writing about
the republic of apples and democracy of oranges. When I see
apples have not become tanks, oranges not bombs,
I know I've not become a slave of words after all.

NOTHING TO DO WITH CROWS

First just one, then a flock
flapping their crooked wings
before me—darkness sweeping the sky.
I watch as if watching a play unfold, a drama of nature.
A single crow is mystery, a flock of crows is fear.
Humans can't escape
the past, the consciousness—the crows
flying within me: witchcraft, prophecy, forbidden awakening.
I sit, limited: I believe what I don't understand,
trust what I don't believe, like a country
built on mistaken foundations constructing a false enemy.
I miss the days of youth, the fence of language
not yet built—only imagining, remembering—
the black crows and white snow opposite but one,
a beauty, a paradox in paradise—to vanish
was to be eternal—I watch now, the crows become fiction,
flying outside me—they're not really there, circling in old silence;
they're not really there, dwelling high on the glassy roofs.

Translations by Ming Di and Neil Aitken

Two Poems

GREEN TO ASH

The no-cloud-at-all sky, the whisper of *never* in weather as in—
           the mind blanks.
                                    Night, that cloud,
but it's hot even under the moon the furrows
lie fallow under, and the dust plumes and plumes,
even the weeds lie flat in the morning,
                          the deep green of the last drop turns a scum
dried black at the tank,

the tank ringed where hope evaporates.

           The birds leave off circling and pant
under the curled leaves of the sagging trees,
                    the sun bare but innocent, everywhere

rippled stalks so light light fills them with empty—

As if some terrible massacre has occurred,
no one goes outdoors.

WARN THE FUTURE

Semaphore and sirens, a fist to the mouth
        to muffle

                                a screeched *No*
while the future's *Yes* models nude.
I'm not looking

at sand screws, a big wind,
a kick through the roof,
bone ache, a bee

                        out of line.
I've got two porches, the insurance of debt,
                the social of insecurity,
forty years of foreshadowing,
                        a prime rate.

                The lower lip quivers—
        who sees the hand at the crypt,
its nails so intent on growing?

            Put shrouds on that boat.

Bloom

The bees are dying toward Beverly Hills
The bees are dying into the sun

At midnight it is day the bees
Of Santa Monica our oranges

Fall sideways toward no beginning the
Bees are dying America in the teeth

By waxlight our bees brim up
From no well they have

Left their reflections on the ice
Of eternity the bees are dying in our

Talk of beginning this young country
Their hives follow the names down

On Alvarado by the light of swans
We go crossing our sunglasses into oblivion

The hands of the Indians are buried
Everywhere nothing grows the feet of the Tongva

Are gathering in white shadows we
Forget them the shadows convulse

We announce ourselves upward into teeth
A cowboy hat without its body the bees

On Sepulveda a wheelchair and silence
In our mouths the sea forgets

We wake our way down the processes
Blooming everywhere the actions of our hands

Sprang —————————————————————————

1 WINTER STARS

You will never forget corpses wrapped in flames—
at dusk, you watched a congregation of crows

gather in the orchard and sway on branches;
in the dawn light, a rabbit moves and stops,

moves and stops along the grass; and as
you pull a newspaper out of a box, glance

at the headlines, you feel the dew on grass
as the gleam of fading stars: yesterday you met

a body-shop owner whose father was arrested,
imprisoned, and tortured in Chile, heard

how men were scalded to death in boiling water;
and, as the angle of sunlight shifts, you feel

a seasonal tilt into winter with its expanse
of stars—candles flickering down the Ganges,

where you light a candle on a leaf and set it
flickering, downstream, into darkness—

dozens of tiny flames flickering into darkness—
then you gaze at fires erupting along the shore.

2 HOLE

No sharp-shinned hawk perches
on the roof rack of his car and scans
for songbirds; the reddening ivy
along a stone wall deepens in hue;
when he picks a sun-gold tomato
in the garden and savors
the burst in his mouth, he catches
a mock-orange spray in the air;
and as he relights the pilot
to a water heater, checks thermostats,
the sound of water at a fountain
is prayer; earlier in the summer,
he watched a hummingbird land,
sip water, and douse its wings,
but, now, a widening hole gnaws
at that time; and, glancing
at a spotted towhee nest on a lintel,
he knows how hunting chanterelles
at the ski basin and savoring
them at dinner is light years away.

3 TALISMAN

Quetzal: you write
        the word on a sheet of paper
                then erase it;

each word, a talisman,
        leaves a track: a magpie
                struts across a portal

and vanishes from sight;
        when you bite into sea urchin,
                ocean currents burst

in your mouth; and when
        you turn, view the white shutters
                to the house,

up the canyon, a rainbow
        arcs into clouds;
                expectations, fears, yearnings—

hardly bits of colored glass
         revolving in a kaleidoscope—
                    mist rising from a hot spring

along a river: suddenly
         you are walking toward Trinity Site
                    searching for glass

and counting minutes
         of exposure under the sun;
                    suddenly small things ignite.

4 *KINTSUGI*

He slips on ice near a mailbox—

no gemsbok leaps across the road—

a singer tapped an eagle feather on his shoulders—

women washed indigo-dyed yarn in this river, but today gallium
    and germanium particles are washed downstream—

once they dynamited dikes to slow advancing troops—

picking psilocybin mushrooms and hearing cowbells in the mist—

as a child, he was tied to a sheep and escaped marauding soldiers—

an apple blossom opens to five petals—

as he hikes up a switchback, he remembers undressing her—

from the train window, he saw they were on ladders cutting fruit off
    cacti—

in the desert, a crater of radioactive glass—

assembling shards, he starts to repair a gray bowl with gold lacquer—

they ate psilocybin mushrooms, gazed at the pond, undressed—

hunting a turkey in the brush, he stops—

from the ponderosa pines: *whoo-ah, whoo whoo whoo*—

5 YELLOW LIGHTNING

In the five a.m. dark, a car with bright lights
and hazard lights blinking drives directly at me;
veering across the yellow lines, I pass by it

and exhale: amethyst crystals accrete
on a string: I will live to see pear
blossoms in the orchard, red-winged black-

birds nesting in the cattails; I love the sighs
you make when you let go—my teeth gripping
your earlobe—pearls of air rising through water—

and as a white moon rising over a canyon
casts pine shadows to the ground, gratitude
rivers through me: sharpened to starlight,

I make our bed and find your crystal
between the sheets; and when I part the curtains,
daylight's a strobe of yellow lightning.

6 RED RUFFED LEMUR

You locate a spotted-towhee nest on a beam,
peony shoots rising out of the earth, but a pang
surges in your blood with each systole—
though spring emerges, the forsythia eludes you—
in a coffee shop, a homeless man gathers
a Chinese magazine and two laundered towels
in a clear plastic bag, mutters "Metro,"
and heads out the door—a bird trills
in the blue spruce, but, when it stops, the silence
is water running out of thawing glacial ice;
and you mix cement in a wheelbarrow,
haul it, in a bucket, up a ladder to a man
on a rooftop plastering a firewall—cherry buds
unfurl along a tidal basin—a red ruffed
lemur squints out of a cage at human faces,
shudders, and scurries back into a hole—
and you surge at what's enfolded in this world:

7 THIS IS THE WRITING, THE SPEAKING OF THE DREAM

Red bougainvillea blooming against the glass—

she likes it when he pulls her to him—

once you saw murres crowding the cliffs of an arctic island—

thousands of blue-black mussels, exposed and gripping rocks at low tide—

he runs his fingers between her toes—

light reflecting off snow dazzles their eyes—

a tiger shark prowls along the shoreline for turtles—

an aspen leaf drops into a creek—

when he tugs the roots of her hair, he begins to tiger—

this is the writing, the speaking of the dream—

no one knows why ten thousands of murres are dying—

he hungers for sunlight to slant along their bodies on a Molokaʻi slope—

sunlight streams as gold-flecked koi roil the waters and churn—

they roil the waters and churn—

killer whales move through Prince William Sound—

8 NET LIGHT

Poised on a bridge, streetlights
on either shore, a man puts
a saxophone to his lips, coins
in an upturned cap; and a carousel

in a piazza begins to turn:
where are the gates to paradise?
A woman leans over an outstretched
paper cup—leather workers sew

under lamps: a belt, wallet, purse—
leather dyed maroon, beige, black—
workers from Seoul, Lagos, Singapore—
a fresco on a church wall depicts

the death of a saint: a friar raises
both hands in the air—on an airplane,
a clot forms in a woman's leg
and starts to travel toward her heart—

a string of notes riffles the water;
and, as the clot lodges, at a market
near lapping waves, men unload
sardines in a burst of argentine light.

9 SPRANG

Before tracking pods of killer whales
in Prince William Sound, she reads a poem

on deck to start each day. In solstice light,
a moose lumbers across a driveway; I mark

orange and purple sea stars exposed at low tide,
the entrance to an octopus den. Astronomers

have observed two black holes colliding;
and, though the waves support relativity,

we need no equation to feel the sprang of space
and time. A marine biologist gives everything

away, weaves her coffin out of alder branches,
lines it with leaves; a carpenter saws kiln-

dried planks to refurbish a porch; I peruse
the tips of honeycrisp apples we planted

last fall, and, though no blossoming appears,
the air is rife with it; the underground

stirs, and I can only describe it by saying
invisible deer move through an orchard in bloom.

Traditional Medicine Shop,
Dachang, 2002.
Photograph by Linda Butler.

The drawers in this medicine cabinet
contain dehydrated roots, flowers,
and parts of animals and fish, as well
as herbs, bark, and other items. The
patient is told to steep the ingredients
in hot water to make a fragrant, or
sometimes acrid-smelling, tea.

While Sick

Still your hands
Still your eyes
Still your ears
Still everything percolating in your mind
Real or non-real
Chattering or muttering
Still everything
Take this moment
To cleanse the stagnation from all the pollution
that's been forced into the body
Spare half of the day from your floating life
Cleanse carefully
painstakingly
devoutly.

Otherwise
Your body will be unable
to pick the flower of the joyful soul

Translation by Ming Di

DANIEL TOBIN

The Way to Jade Mountain _____

after Li Bai, for Shujen Wang

1 UPSTREAM, DOWNSTREAM

I steered the river against its current,
dawn a brightly colored veil of mist

where the gorges rose like palace walls,
a thousand miles up, a thousand back

until nightfall, and heard from both banks
the monkeys' numberless, deafening cries

behind my boat, now always with me,
the ten thousand mountains coming to pass.

2 MOUNTAIN TEMPLE

Tonight, to make this mountain my home,
a temple's tall tower edging the cliff,

I'll reach my hand with the same gesture,
a man standing tiptoe from a ladder's height

who would pluck the living fruit of the stars.
But let me be quiet, catch the stillness

less than a whisper, less than a breath,
for fear I'll disturb the people of heaven.

3 NEITHER HERE, NOR THERE

I've been staring so long at my face
in my wine—suddenly it's dusk.

A blizzard of dogwood blossoms
has fallen, making my clothes a dune.

I'm so drunk I walk out into
the stream, the moon there, the sky.

The birds, I think, must be far away,
like everybody else. Except me.

4 SITTING ALONE

Birds are flying in great rings out there,
it looks like where sky thins into space;

out there, where a lone cloud is floating
like someone without anyplace to go.

We look at each other, the mountain
and me, as though we'd do so forever.

Until it welcomes me under its shelter.
Until there is nothing else but the mountain.

Dogtrack

I won't ask foolish questions, such as
Why must the dog run?
It could refuse to run.

I also won't ask, for instance,
Why pursue a mechanical bunny?
It could refuse to go faster.

The song of progress blares out loud
It is the work of machines to wear the animals down.
I, too, ran on that track, sunning away my childhood,
Now the grind of work pummels and pulls me apart.

The gate flies opens, and someone
Keeps striking the starting gong, a beehive. Women sit wearing hats,
    even late at night,
I sit too, ten fingers tapping my keyboard
A greyhound in its sandpit, legs pounding round its circuit, its hell.

As if those on the field were just waiting for the show to end,
As if they were to curve into a question mark and that was the answer,
As if the world were only black and white,
Only owners and workers, gamblers and gawkers.

In their World of Difference, they perform their noisy pantomime.
As for us, their loyal friends,
When we ask for a response, they lift a leg.

Translation by Jeremy Tiang

The Man Who Cuts Firewood for the Winter

The man who cuts firewood for the winter
brings more life to us
than the low-lying sun.
The man who cuts firewood for the winter
is quick and precise with his hands—
the way he cuts wood astonishes me.

As the cold weather approaches,
the man who cuts firewood
is more patient than the season over his shoulder.
He is calm and focused

—then the ax comes down. Even more
than a revolution, it prevents me
from writing.

I look out and see him in the yard
as he straightens up, then
departs.
I know he can survive the winter,
more than the winter.

Translation by Ming Di and Frank Stewart

Two Poems _____

AND THE BIRDS GUIDE US

A dewdrop hangs on the lip of an orchid
A volcano rumbles in another ether

Something has hit us
And we don't know why

It's April. The prairie
Is brewing a new blizzard

Cornfields adrift in the whiteout wind
One-legged cranes darken the braided river

Rings of ice like shackles
And the sky in an origami dream

At the fork of the road I stand in blindfold
Lines of hexagrams, form of the formless

This light and shadow— it's all energy
Same difference in the field of perception

Every tomorrow has two handles
Every seed contains its own fortune

This is the truth to those who still trust
A thread so thin, unbreakable

Fire from the sea and into the sea—the Big
Island—ash from the womb of the earth

Children of the rivers and mountains
We carry a dream as ancient as the cranes

Sailing across the sky, ocean and desert
Uttering a cry that's almost too human

The birds have moved on
And the fields still aquiver with their spirits

They do not think   they live
Simply   each day a small gift

THE OLD MAN SPEAKS OF PARADISE AT
TWIN CITIES: A GHAZAL

Do not move. Let me speak of a river in paradise
A turquoise gift from fiery stars that is paradise

How do you measure a river's weight, color, smell, touch?
How do you feel the veins of sand in a breathing paradise?

Eons of earth story, long before rocks, plants or bones
Bulging with flesh and blood in every corner of paradise

You call me Old Man, 12,000 years old, but really I'm a baby of
River Warren, swollen with glacier water flooding the paradise

My torso sloughed by old ice, two cities on sandstone bluffs
Headwaters of a 2350-mile road towards the gulf of paradise

A walk along the beach, a bag of rocks, fossils and agates
Each tells stories of the river, land & life—a kinship of paradise

Come to me at dawn or dusk, by foot, canoe or a single shell
To greet eagles, cranes, fox, trees . . . a ten-mile gorge of paradise

Gar, bass, goldeye, redhorse, bowfin, stoneroller, buffalo, drum, sunfish
Sickleback, darter, walleye, dace, mooneye . . . in the waves of paradise

The St. Anthony Fall that walked up 10 miles from Fort Snelling
Clams and shells in Kasota stones—layered history of paradise

Put your fingers into the bluff, and pull a handful of sand
From the Ordovician sea, each perfect to make a paradise

From time to time, I take you into the amniotic womb
A reminder of our origin from a black, red, white, blue paradise

Do not dam me. To move freely is to evolve is to live
Lock feeds fear feeds hate feeds violence to the base of paradise

The Mississippi, temple on earth, home of all living things
Would you tread with love, through the heart of paradise?

We are water—H_2O—two hands under an open heart
Pulsing, dissolving, bonding the earth to a green paradise

Stop seeking before or after life, for a paradise
Already in us, in each cell of being that is paradise

Qutang Gorge Entrance, Daixi, 2003.
Photograph by Linda Butler.

Chinese anthropologists believe that
Daixi village, near the confluence of
the Daixi tributary and the Yangtze,
was inhabited thirty-five hundred
years ago. In 2003, the village was
destroyed and the residents relocated.

WANG YIN

Two Poems

THREE PINES GROW ON A NORTHERN SEASHORE

three pines grow on a northern seashore
strong winds constrain their height
like hair under the constant scissoring of a barber
these pines grow horizontally, flat-crowned

beach. ocean. lighthouse. coastline
only three stubby pines
these trees of the cold zone
sprout huge cones on their dark branches

high heels leave deep divots in the sand
summertime and boys are under the trees casting fishhooks
that headless fish and those seashells flung
upon the shore can never return to the sea

I don't know how these pines on this northern shore
might look in the winter
or if the mussels will still be dying on the beach
or if the gray waves will still be striking the feet of these trees

I know only that far away, in the East
dreaming of my love, I may someday
lower my head and suddenly remember these three pines
on the wild shores of Brittany

THIS IS THE BLACKEST BLACK

This is the blackest black
I cannot see through this darkness to
the sand on top of my feet
nor can I see the wavering shadows
Only dense stars like grains of salt
floating overhead

After yesterday, before tomorrow,
every day marked by the same mistakes
and endlessly repeating
their radiance
their fugitive radiance
Their fugitive and unreliable radiance
has already set out

Rapidly accelerating, flickering specks, are they
speeding airships
or the silent whispering of
interstellar space itself
perpetually hot as lightning
and cold as fire

If the starry sky surrounding the dust and us
was suddenly rent apart
if it all collapsed without warning
the nameless Buddhas in the caves
would not feel any pain
Those headless Buddhas
cannot be conquered again
It is only we who can never again be ourselves
poets Duo Duo, Jian Zhao, Lan Lan, Ye Zhou, and I

Translations by Andrea Lingenfelter

Two Poems

FAT GRAY SQUIRRELS

flee from me like furry sine waves—
    bushy inchworms—eyebrows
        skating over speedbumps
            on the forest floor. They leap

            onto the backs of trees, and—brown
      bark flying—ride them up to green-
   haired limbs where they curse me
with sounds like monkeys gibbering,

macaws screeching, cats hair-balling.
    Whump! Whump! Whump!
        their emphysemic coughing prays.
            And when I tire of them, and leave—

        Choonk, choonk, choonk, choonk!
      Hohnh, hohnh, hohnh, hohnh!—
they thank their Squirrel God for driving me

away.

HOUSE CENTIPEDE

My first one looked, as gray dawn crawled
                      across my eyes, like a chorusline
of spiders on the ceiling, set to fall
            and fang me in my bed. No wonder
I submerged the monster in a *Black Flag* slough.

Anything so multi-legged and bristly
                     had to have a horror-name: *Death's Head
Hell-Dangler,* say, or *Septic Shadow-Creeper.*
              Who'd have guessed *house centipede,*
as if each house comes, cozy, with its own?

Alien as the gulper eel (all mouth
                    and dangling tapeworm gut), house
centipedes could have crash-landed
           on Earth, speaking in isotopes of oxygen.
What relief, H.C., to crack open

California Bugs, and find you
                 are a shy recluse, harmless to humans,
though deadly to spiders: your favored prey.
            Small savior who, traversing the TV
like a one-bug parade, made my son

annunciate, "Daddy! Him!"—death
               to the black widow and brown recluse.
Long live your rowing legs, your speed
           when startled, whirring quick as a breeze
across the carpet when, up for a midnight sip,

I flick the light. (Don't crawl too close
              to my bed, please.) May your hunting
prosper, frilled protector. May you fatten
          on my enemies. May we share this house
in peace.

Necropastorals _____

1

Disruption of the warblers' routes   Parched white hair
Of brome and grama

Conifers retreating upslope   Dominion
Of the dry white oak

The woods propose a blind white room   then burn

2

A white   accessible

          Only through green   A black
          Contracted

               As a plague

               Of fern fronds chokes
               This gully

Not yet bone
No longer crisp

               Root threads inching down the colorspace

               From succulent
               To dread

3

When no human person's here
The pine woods brim with sound
Rare in the galaxy

It matters

Crabgrass silts a drainage ditch
With pointless green
My word for sacred is undisturbed

4

Beneath the earth's skin lies
                    A face   Black oak knuckles

Clench it   Citizens have sieved
                        Down through it

                        To the soil
                        Dead seeds swollen black   laxing

                        Where the blind-eyed beetles
                        Harvest rot for keep

5

The white pine's

                        Awl might strike and wake
                        The blinded face

                        Long sentences of cadmium and acids
                        Scribbled on the wetlands

A profanity vital in the otter's mouth
                        Who sine-waves over ice fields with his death

Already messaged in his spine
                        Wedged between his ribs a gift

                        (The gift a flaw the flaw a wound)
                        From which his blood's black liquor flows

                        A second body running out
                        Across the smoking snow

6

Look inside the box to think outside the box

Boxes made for holding goods or corpses
Corpsewood boxes made from clearcuts

Nothing's clear in a denuded landscape
But nobody's looking as shadows clock over footpaths

On a football afternoon with the light
Going out of the sky
Earlier and earlier

And the bluescreened faces
Of the fiercest predators the earth has ever seen
Pretend to a devastating mildness

There's such a thing in the world now
As "nature deficit disorder"
Which means it may be too late

As names make boxes to hold the memories of things
That have almost finished vanishing

7

If my need were less dire I'd be assailed
By less silence
                        Here among the beardtongue
And strawberry clover   Otters cottontails hawks jays loves

Why have you savaged your faces
Against me
          (Rapacious Pilgrims ghosting
Overgrass   I hear you passing
And the skins of the dead you wore)
                                        If I were less human
You could be more so   I made a botch
But didn't blare it   which ought

To count
                  And who am I now What waste
Have I assembled and is it part of me
This rat's long tail

8

The asshole trees shit seeds
Which fuck the darkness underground

Sucking till the wet threads come

Death in its other aspect
The series' prequel

Waste light vomited in pools

To stink and bleed
Into delicate fringes

9

When the woods stand empty there will be no woods
And incarnation's a tensioned wire
Will warp and straighten and its pain
Will never end

The Terror

Alas poor things! how well do I remember the pain it gave me, to be thus obliged to pass and execute sentence upon them. John James Audubon

A tiny island off Labrador, thronged
with nesting seabirds. The scrape
of boots, hobbed with heavy nails for grip
on the slick sea rocks. Gunfire and alarms,
a tempest of wings and cries: Audubon
and his team are collecting specimens.
Out of the riot one Arctic Tern dives
toward a stunned young man, William Ingalls,
young medic, who normally remains
aboard ship; and the tern lands, cringing
in the instep of his boot. Audubon notices
three things at once: the tern; the involuntary
gesture Ingalls makes—bending forward,
hands half-reached, as if to help the bird; and—
flushed in a burst from his memory—
himself, eight years old, his younger sister,
father and stepmother in prison in Nantes,
1793. Stone walls and floor, iron hinges.
He hears outside the barked command,
the synchronized report of muskets, and knows
from having seen it, what happens next:
smoke from the muzzles, and the body slumps
against the wall. Now he is looking
from the eyes of the tern looking at him,
to the eyes of Ingalls, looking at him.
Audubon recoils, steels himself, reloads.
Later he'll describe the day's shooting
in his *Ornithological Biography.*
Later he'll tell Ingalls there was nothing
the young man could do to help.

Two Poems

SEABIRDS

Sometimes the sea meanders to the land, folded as a seagull.
Sometimes the land walks to the sea, hiding in a boat.
The sea and land go deeper to each other through rain and lightning.
In the clouds, seagulls measure things.
In the waves, boats do too.
When it's quiet and calm, the sea stops on your fingertips
looking at you,
and then flies away like a cup of water poured
but retrieving itself when you start to care, even just slightly, about worldly matters.

Seagulls gather their wings, boats their sails.
With the rise and fall of tides, the nobleman's gray hair gets long
and the beauty's mirror gets thin

while crowds of white-robed monks rush to the sunrise
and pods of black whales to the sunset.

Translation by Ming Di

WATCHING CROWS IN THE SUMMER PALACE

Like leaves spinning into the sky,
like black-robed monks reciting
obscure sutras, I look up.
Across the desolate water divided by the lake's banks

there is a secluded corner
west of the bustling royal garden.
As if dedicated to this bleak winter,
crows protest above my head.

The whole afternoon, I sit at the lakeside, alone,
clap my hands and watch crows launch from treetops
flinging their lugubrious ideas over the limpid sky
as if they were bills from hell requiring payment

in the human world. They plunge
like an aspiration mauled by life.
I know they will invade my dreams
demanding words from me
to praise the darkness.

Translation by Ming Di and Rachel Galvin

Food Is Running Out

Food is running out
I have to tell you
what we are facing
Corn, wheat, potatoes
and rice, all these we live on
but never produce are gone. Hunger comes
like the fireworks you've never seen
Hunger is the food tomorrow gives us today
But before it's completely dark
and the sun not set, the mountains are already black
Don't say this is the last banquet
where you need to be dressed up
Don't say the knives and forks and plates
are just being manufactured
Before the moon has come out, we
have an opportunity to be opportunists
We can step into the autumn rice fields
in the South, or the storms
There will always be a way to the distant warehouse
There will always be robbers and a furious judge
There will always be coffins and verses of praise
There will always be rice when we wake up from sleep
in the properties stolen by the mouse
in the lullabies the peasants are no longer singing
in the hands of the beggars, between their fingers
The rice will fly up with the ghosts of our ancestors, and
land in a paddy field of moist words
All night, in the darkness
surrounded by fatigue, I wait

for one word after another to sprout
Before they open up, flowering, growing into
great lines on Du Fu's mustaches,
or clear moonlight in Li Bai's glass—
I pick them up and quickly stuff them into my mouth
Food is running out
I stretch out my hands and turn to Time
I know I'm more hungry than the rice granary
and more fatigued—will you cry for me

Translation by Ming Di

Qutang Gorge Entrance II, Daixi, 2003.
Photograph by Linda Butler.

In June 2003, when the reservoir
formed, the confluence of the Daixi
tributary and the Yangtze River
disappeared beneath the waters,
which washed over the feet of the
distant mountains. The ruins of
Daixi town also vanished.

I Swallow an Iron Moon

I'm swallowing an iron moon,
a screw they call it.
I'm swallowing industrial wastewater, unemployment,
and orders.
People die young, who are shorter than the machines.
I'm swallowing migration, displacement,
skywalks and rusty life.
I can't swallow any more. All that I've swallowed rushes out
of my throat
spreading like a shameful poem
on my fatherland.

Translation by Ming Di

Three Poems

DUSK

The pony kicks the stump in the stable,
The fish thrashes in the basket,
The dog barks in the yard,
How they love and cherish themselves,
The very source of pain,
The still pulse of the moon,
The ceaseless river...

A GIFT

The leaf, not resisting, falls,
And when the wind

Spins it around again,
It rustles, without resisting.

In its tiny wizened body, love breathes
More passionately than when on the tree.

Yes, I will not die,
A gift from these leaves.

TWILIGHT

When a child, from the riverbank:
The sun a slow ember over water.
Grown up, my entombment in it
Will surely not hurt
The light well of my being.

Certainly I can live more delicately,
Say, in an old urn on the wall stump
Covered by dried grass,
A tiny eye in the lid of that container,
That thin beam of twilight, dusk.

Translations by Stephen Haven and Li Yongyi

Shoe Repair, Old Zigui, 2003.
Photograph by Linda Butler.

When Zigui's downtown was destroyed,
this shoemaker constructed a shack of
salvaged materials. He had come to the
town seeking work. To discourage poor
migrants like him, the government pro-
hibited them from becoming legal citizens
and enrolling their children in school.

YANG KE

Two Poems

WALKING TOWARDS FLOWER MOUNTAIN (SUITE)

*Translator's Note: Flower Mountain (Huashan) is in Ningming County,
Guangxi province, along Mingjiang River. Around 1,500 rough-edged
human figures, bursting with raw vitality, are painted on a cliff face in
cinnabar. The largest of the figures is three meters tall, and the shortest is
around thirty centimeters. The figures are spread over an area about fifty
meters high and nearly two hundred meters wide. This place is widely
thought to be the cultural fountainhead of the Zhuang Minority.*

1

Hey-yo hey-yo—
I am a paean in blood   I am a tribute to fire
From the tip of a boar's tusk I came
From a pheasant's fluffed-up feathers I came
From strange power of bone ornaments I came
Having snuffed out the ravenous glow in a wolf's eyes I came
Having faced down the flaming stripes on a tiger's brow I came
From a straight arrow and a stout bow I came here
Stepping over death agonies of my prey
Hey-yo blood   *hey-yo* fire
Hey-yo fierce beauty
With sword raised   beating a drum   to a gong's beat I came
—Ni-lo!
. . .
From nodding ears of millet I came
From corn tassels lit up by sunlight I came
From ravines and garden strips no wider than a conical hat
To the whiz of a full-swung machete blade I came
By power of flames to clear planting grounds I came
Hey-yo blood   *hey-yo* fire
Hey-yo for ripe, bursting beauty
With joyful songs   hopping like sparrows   we come dancing
A bride tosses an embroidered ball in our wake

Red-dyed eggs smack shell-to-shell as we come
Barn-houses of spotted and yellow bamboo rise at our heels
We carefully press rice cakes in family molds
Steam from our five kinds of rice wafts downwind
We are a paean in blood   We are a tribute to fire
Hey-yo blood   *hey-yo* fire
Hey-yo for beauty of things exalted

2

A series of arrowheads aimed at the blood-red sun   loosed
At a wild bull with eyes as red as the sun
A mountain man of Luoyue clad in rawhide
Bellows straight from his rawhide-clad soul
His bellow is like that of a red-eyed fighting bull
Sounds of his own footsteps cheer him on
All across the wild slopes…he steps over
Moans of companions fallen in bamboo thickets
The might of his arm
Drives the shaft of his spear
Straight into a leopard's mouth

The cliff seethes with raging blood
Wind whips past the forest trees
Past the heart's flapping banner

Luscious smells of evening
Hang over a hearth fire
Snapping of green firewood
Shoots up sparks to join stars in the sky
Sending up tales of Old Buloto,* who fought Thunder King
And of Mother Le's visit to heaven
And dreams of a feathered man

*Legendary progen-
itor of the Zhuang
minority*

The embers long ago died down
Now only this timeless message
Still blazes across the cliff face
More primitive than pictographic signs
More sacred than the sun

3

Even the wind was massacred
Gutted moorlands   final resting place
Of skulls that kissed the sword   blood that drenched arrows
Corpses puddled in blood
Hoof-pounding melee now recumbent
Clanging massacre   blades hacking flesh
Outright cruelty or cold torture
Rising crescendo of war gongs
Summoning bows and swords   summoning rattan shields
Not despairing even when mothers wail
From ruins of established tribes
Youthful stockades sprang up
By way of more deaths   barbarity led the way to civilization
Oh the maiden who sounded a drum with her severed arm
Was passed down in folk songs
Worshipped as the heroine of her people

Although cooking smoke was severed by sharp blades
Some found a riverbank where it could grow rankly
A marsh once soaked in blood
Cast off the heroic era of brass drums
Yet never once did war turn rusty
Blood in grim and vivid hues
Sinful and holy, washed over the land

Through wind-whipped waves   past sails torn to pieces
Step into a canoe that hoists no sail
Track the bear wounded by an arrow   its trickle of blood
Run toward the hunter who wears a quiver
Turn toward offerings of netted fish
Turn toward offerings flushed from thickets
Beauty of nakedness   of yielding warmth

Pent-up blood dissipates in time   whitecaps sweep away loneliness
From loftiest peaks   torrents of love race down
Once-tempting dilemmas fade away in time
Young hearts were ignited by an embroidered ball

GREAT MIGRATION

Raise—it—overhead

Carry that urn of fragrant wine overhead
Raise those sealed-away seasons above shoulder height
With trembling arms
Swaying like a mountain beech to gasping breaths
Oh waterfall of wine
It tilts
Spills
That reddish-brown flame with such enlivening power
Gives way to a suffocating blueness
Now a hearthstone's column of smoke   rises apart from others

In pieces now   that rugged old urn shaped by quiet toil

Here, white is the
color of mourning.

There is a white-colored farewell*
Streamers flapping on the trail
From high on the mountain
Pouring down
Into the valley
Rising and falling like waves
Wordless, subdued gaze of the whole village
The whole village watches, wordless and subdued
Adrift at a creeping pace
A gravestone as silent as a cliff face
Now an unvisited island
The love tale of troll with naiad becomes possible

Crow of rooster, bark of dog, moo of cow, shout of woman,
     tang of fish, reek of goat, smell of sweat, fragrance of rice
Scatter like mist

†*The Redwater River*
Planning Report said,
"In order to construct
a terraced series of ten
hydropower stations
according to plan,
240,000 inhabitants
were relocated."

Ughhh...
Off toward the sun and higher ridges, to the crashing of gongs
History of squatting burial, of tattoos and shorn-headed vows
Forever left behind on the cliffs, forever
Descendants of Buloto
Following the course of Redwater River†
In the direction
Of a requiem
They go forward

Translations by Denis Mair

Bayou Cul-de-Sac,
Ocean Springs, MS, 2005.
Photograph by Linda Butler.

The owners of upscale homes lived on
a bayou more than three miles from
the Gulf of Mexico, never expecting
their neighborhood could be destroyed
by a storm. But Katrina's massive
waves shattered these homes.
Only one owner rebuilt.

Three Poems

GRAIN BUDS

Facing watery light and shadow, afternoon's
fitful breezes lose their way among the branches
A waxbill flies down from the roof
flits past, halting at
my brimming basin of water
forces himself to calm his boundless astonishment
Like a lonely moment in a dream, on an unfamiliar
last patch of soil, he sips nervously
My weary heart starts beating wildly
A broken drum sounding seven paces away

Translation by Andrea Lingenfelter

PINE GARDEN

The time I turned and saw the twilight darkening
and behind the first stars on the horizon, the quiver of Sagittarius
brightened and in front of me a thick layer of pine needles
and on both sides of the quiver, glowing agate and fine jade
      This was not the whole mystery. In the distance
      hills pleaded with me to stay, streams were unwilling to let me go

Once, I coursed down a meandering trail like a silent river
looked up and counted the tender green needles of pines
From among those graceful trees the night set free
fireflies and from the sky, a wide and perfect ripeness descended
      with nerve ending keen beyond compare, touching
      and caressing. See how heavy the dew is on grasses

Moonlight, late rising on a tranquil night, envelops the pond
to see its own reflection, shines in the center
Suppose I say we too were once like unsleeping fish listening
to the night, surely after the tide of pines subsided
      perhaps moving, dimly, with the shadows of reeds and cattails
      toiling unceasingly between heaven and earth

As to the two ends of the scale: memory and total forgetfulness
Facts show no space divides them: a larva rolls over in a dream
wakes up a red turtledove, who swallows it whole; all the while
birds of a different species call to one another in duet
      Darting sunlight above the forest floor, painting and
      poetry change the invisible into the whole secret

Translation by Michelle Yeh and Frank Stewart

FRAGMENT

A wild goose dives into the ancient pool
Life sinks within
Nameless ravine, lonely fruit
Holding primal peace in the deep mysterious confusion
A man picking flowers among reeds abruptly raises his head
to catch sight of a flock of vultures
A pine fire burns on the clear lot
A small tribe
guarded by a hundred vultures
through misty rain, plagues, and superstitions
A tribe of buried totems and taboos
I have seen it once—behind the mountain
across the spring, a tribe in the heart of the jungle
where rebellion and slaughter once took place
Its entire history is an episode of regret

The wind is time sighing, fiery twilight on water
as red as the timeless blood behind the mountain
I lean against a giant tree
that resembles memory, so old
and stern but still
sustaining me, allowing me to sigh
to feel its growth and helplessness
and pass on the legend about a small tribe that once lived.

Translation by Michelle Yeh and Lawrence R. Smith

YANG SENJUN

Untitled

Horses—they run
faster than wind
but fast horses—
they run
within the
wind

Translation by Ming Di

YAO FENG

Untitled ———————————————————————

a bird uncovers the sky to show what he has collected
— the clouds are all in the sky, in the cage

a bud swaying in the breeze, says:
I will blossom if you'll be a bee!

a wave takes me and asks
if a stranded whale can be dragged back to sea
a tree pulls out its roots, waves its wig to bid farewell
then runs away to some far-flung place

a mountain leads me to the cliff
turns around to offer me the gift of an abyss

the tour guide says that tourists are the best people in this city
then he brings me to the casino for gambling and fun

Translation by Kit Kelen and Fang Xia

YU XIAOZHONG

Two Poems

RIVER QI

Translator's Note: The River Qi, pronounced chi, *is one of the thousand tributaries of the Yangtze River in Hubei province. Located upstream, the Three Gorges Dam is the world's largest hydroelectric-power station. In China, people are not allowed to talk about the dam's construction, which displaced millions, caused natural disasters, damaged the environment, and destroyed the oldest archaeological sites in the country.*

A river you can sail along
is more than just a river
especially when you can sail
with the flow—the sailing
and flowing become one stream.

How long has it been like this?
Not long.
Damaged and ruined for thirty years.
Or sixty years.
All nature's agonies converge here
in the river of grief
that raises the riverbed,

A small tributary of the Yangtze.
A small stream of a bigger phenomenon.
Many rivers run into the same fate.
Many rivers pour out their sadness
as if the sadness upstream
isn't sad enough,

as if I've been speaking speaking nonstop
with a retarded mind: if only…if only…
Well, let me say it once again. If only I can sail a boat
back to my old home
even if I inadvertently fall into water, choking,
jerking about, and swearing,

I will say to you loudly: Hello stranger,
if you ever come to River Qi, please sail with me
against the tides.

WITNESSING DAOISM

In my balcony, there's a bird-dropping
on the iron rails.
I will not clean it off
out of respect for flying creatures.
I will not clean it
off.
I will even take it
as a flower
on rust.

Translations by Ming Di and Kerry Shawn Keys

YU XIUHUA

Two Poems

ON THE THRESHING FLOOR, I CHASE CHICKENS AWAY

And I see sparrows fly over. They look around
as if it's inappropriate to stop for just any grain of rice.
They have clear eyes, with light inside.
Starlings also fly over, in flocks, bewildered.
They flutter and make a sound that seems to flash out light.
When they're all gone, the sky gets lower, in dark blue.
In this village deep in the central plains,
the sky is always low, forcing us to look at its blue,
the way our ancestors make us look inside ourselves,
narrow and empty, so we look out again
at the full September—
we're comforted by its insignificance but hurt by its smallness.
Living our life this way, we feel secure.
So much rice. Where does it come from?
So much gold color. Where does it come from?
Year after year I've been blessed, and then deserted.
When happiness and sadness come in the same color code, I'm happy
to be forgotten. But who am I separated from?
I don't know. I stay close to my own hours.

CROSSING HALF OF CHINA TO SLEEP WITH YOU

To sleep with you or to be slept with, what's the difference if there's any?
Two bodies collide—the force, the flower pushed open by the force,
the virtual spring in the flowering—nothing more than this,
and this we mistake as life restarting.
In half of China, things are happening: volcanoes
erupting, rivers running dry,
political prisoners and displaced workers abandoned,
elk deer and red-crowned cranes shot.
I cross the hail of bullets to sleep with you.
I squeeze many nights into one morning to sleep with you.
I run across many of me and many of me run into one to sleep with you.
Of course I can be misled by butterflies
and mistake praise as spring,
a village similar to Hengdian as home.
But all these are absolutely indispensable reasons that I sleep
with you.

Translation by Ming Di

Four Poems

ASSOCIATION OF ABSOLUTE AESTHETICS

I squat down, waiting to hear
an earthworm, thin as a shoelace, speak.

By my side is a field of knee-high canola.
I lay down my bike. There seems to be no way to get lost out here.

Everybody, once grown up, claims
they have not seen a talking worm.

The world is small enough, but still
you can't find what you really want.

Mr. Earthworm, do you know what you desire
most? The string of your body

looks very short, like an invitation
for us to use you as bait.

And your slender figure, very suitable for a tango underground.
This is also why I respect you.

I have more patience for you than
I have for my own life.

I don't care about your gender. If I ask you to be my muse,
do you care that this poem is so clean, without any mud?

Translation by Ming Di and Neil Aitken

THE BOOKS OF THE ORIGINAL ROLE

Years ago my body missed me.
This shouldn't have happened, but in fact
did, many times. My body is my miracle,
which sounds presumptuous, but what I was thinking
was how miracles constrain my freedom, and even
constitute another form of corruption. My body hanging there,
like a ripe apple that could fall at any time.
You know, if it strikes you on your head by chance
the world will probably crack open, awakening.
I lay on my side on the grass, surrounded by the thoughts
of summer insects. I like things with a rhythm.
On the grass, the insects thought rhythmically without tuning.
Following that rhythm, it seemed as if I'd seized
fate by its Achilles' heel.
I'd brought a half-bottle of wine, the beef jerky I was chewing
full of the yak's life. I was grinding down my own body
which would not miss me anymore. My body
was once the three yaks who had just emerged from the valley.
There, the snow streams on the Aba were like clear strings
that had melted the memory of hard granite stones.
My body missed me, meaning that from the beginning
my body was a composition of bodies
from a man and the one who returns from death.
They've brought me joys that contradicted each other like the truth.
However, what is blind is never the body itself.
You know, I could have explained this much better.

Translations by Ming Di and Neil Aitken

PRIMER FOR MY BROTHER ANTS

Whenever I wore black clothes
in the most ecstatically colorful places
your little silhouettes were everywhere.
The sigh of black silk is always lurking in
the secret stitching, and never
is there a lack of delicate black veils
dedicated to bone-hard work. In dream country,
black muscles bar the brawny
star-vault of love. Even my demanding heart
did not imagine my final escape would be
so primitive. I don't know if I should
apologize a bit because for so long
I have had these strange feelings
for you. I want to step over the chasm
between us. Suddenly, strangely,
and for no reason I publicly declare
you my brother. Around me, the spring wind
decimates; now, there are few ideal
specimens left to observe.
There is something in you
blacker than a specter. There is not one day
in the year when you aren't rehearsing
the essence of being. Your tenaciousness
is so black, it makes frightening shades
feel a nameless sadness. Some petals
have started to fall, but the landscape in April
still reminds me of immense breasts.
You are blind, but it is your blindness
that draws you to your purpose.
When you move, you are like strokes of calligraphy
writing the encyclopedia of heaven under my feet.

Translation by Tony Barnstone and Denise Wong Velasco

MUSHROOM SERIES

Pessimists rarely fall in love with mushrooms,
or like you, stay truthful to the physical sensations.
Common sense tells you that unless you betray the Nihilism
you wouldn't be interested in the spirit of mushrooms—
they roll and tumble better than bodies.

They rock 'n' roll in the pan and wheel into your mouth,
tender and fresh, least afraid of being exploited.
Any truth that optimists can think of, they present it
in a shape. Anything you want to conceal,
they perform the profoundest pardon.

They have smelt the taste of little chickens.
They love garlics when they sign a contract with broccolis.
They open their parachutes and fall, till landing in you
and becoming small nutritious gods.
The difference between disappearance and digestion

may not be as big as you thought. Before disappearing,
one of them from inside you will hand out a new recipe
asking you to be more patient next time in tasting
what mushrooms imply. There has never been anything
closer to what the universe implies than mushrooms.

Translation by Ming Di

Poem Written with Buson _____

He told us
to go outside

and if someone talked to us
to be silent

not in a hostile way
more like after the bells

have stopped performing
more like the building

glazed with sun
no longer heard

in evening wind
he stumbles suddenly

it's because they have voted
to stop thinking

life can be taken away
Girls from Ohara

owls darkening
the maples at evening

I have never been
on a difficult journey

my beloved village
no longer satisfies me

the white flower
in the darkness of the heart

the gateway at midnight
someone goes through

to become invisible
in the capital

when the lanterns of finance
have been extinguished

the two of them
feel strengthened

by wine and the songs
that make the path

that can only
be seen in darkness

hours later the rustling
of her robe

says an old well
is a frightening thing

ZHAI YONGMING

from *Following Huang Gongwang through the Fuchun Mountains*

Translator's Note: The Fuchun Mountains are in a lush area near Hang-zhou, Zhejiang province. They were immortalized by the Yuan Dynasty painter Huang Gongwang (1269–1354) in his famous landscape scroll Dwelling in the Fuchun Mountains. *The following poems are from Zhai Yongming's book-length sequence based on the scroll. The opening line of "Poem Twenty" is from a letter by the Liang Dynasty literati Wu Jun (469–520), who traveled in the area. The poem in the third stanza of "Poem Twenty" is by the southern Song Dynasty poet Lu You (1125–1209).*

POEM TEN

Dusk descends, the path sometimes hidden, sometimes revealed:
a single tree, a solitary figure, a weightless leaf,
a cave of fish, a brook of green, a stone of brittleness,
A bird understands the silence

The master appears, imaginary footsteps cross a stone bridge
He and I brush past each other
a distance of several thousand years

Alternations appear   on lofty ridges and towering mountains,
    sometimes hidden, sometimes revealed
I brush past Beauty
And miss it by thousands of years

Balance is revealed   grand courtyards and tiny huts like
    steelyard weights
bear down on   the weight of donkeys and people
like so many half-sensed doubts and suspicions
Everything has cause and effect   even powerful brushstrokes
The first pose always precedes the final pose

The same mountains, the same road
the same geography, paying respects to nature
paying respects to the crimson and green tinted heights
It crawls along between every seam in the paper
large trees and small, all gazing upward
A person of ancient times and a person of today, one in front and
    one behind
Following Huang Gongwang, walking in and walking out
experiencing a spell of presence

POEM FIFTEEN

Crimson spring festival,   Dragons! Phoenixes! float into view
Crimson   is a modern color
China is red———————solitary, brittle facepaint
is what you need

Fireworks rain down forlornly, faintly visible are the sky-shattering
    cannons of economic depression
War, the shadow of war reappears
a few madmen making noise at
every node of the internet   hopping around
PM 2.5 smog swallows up the ancient realm
"To walk upon the paper is to have oxygen to breathe"

Spread a cloth, take out a paperweight
Breath held in rapt attention, let me
poke my head into Huang Gongwang's three-layered space:

Mountains and rivers dense and lush, the most primordial
Before we came, this place was formless, unseen
These mountains and rivers didn't need a first draft, they were
    completely refined
Before footsoles tread upon them, green moss enrobed them
Gaze like a fine brush   deftly flourished
Brush and ink like breathing
Brush flows like dancing
Beasts, flowers, and birds suspended beside the ancients

Green colored haze colored paper
Setting down memories
The first layer like floating filaments   the second layer like powder

the third and fourth layers stroked gently like skin
the fifth and sixth layers fragrant like orchids
the seventh and eighth layers absorb sunlit rivers and mists and haze
the ninth layer bores between my eyes   transformed into energy

POEM TWENTY

"Fuyang to Tonglu   is one hundred–some li"

I'm driving my car, new willows lining the banks, oblivious
No clamoring cicadas, no gibbons
All I see are newly built suburbs and government-issue farmhouses
Wind and mist don't cleanse
Sky and mountains clash
The Peach Blossom Spring remains
as happy   as muddled   as ever

Fishing poles gone, conversations gone
That strong young man has moved to town
His old parents   at loose ends
their hearts troubled, yet mountains and waters are lucid
Of old, how many sighs and epiphanies
sent how many poets treading among the clouds
Mountains and rivers at once sunlit and clouded
It makes me sigh   O in a reverie
quietly sweeping past Seven Mile Strand

Walking in the mountains in the rain, to Pine Wind Pavilion, suddenly
   the clouds part
A scroll hinting at the "broken ink" of Li Yingqiu, and displaying the tints
   of the Generals Li

The distance of a footstep is Huang Gongwang's history
Green mountains, green history, who will bear witness?
Now, then
Meticulous symmetry, exquisite artistry

Translations by Andrea Lingenfelter

ZHANG ER

Buji River Serenade

The Buji River, a tribu-
tary of the Shenzhen
River, runs through
Shenzhen, in Guang-
dong province, one of
China's most pros-
perous cities.

Sunset, gray rain, and railroad tracks blockaded by the river
Power lines gather concentrated daylight, clouds grow dim
till they are swallowed by boundless silence
as if they had sunk into a counterfeit continent

Someone meditates while jogging on the other side
maintaining the standard for an outsider's sense of shame
afterwards, an even longer negotiation
like a golden retriever that has gone missing and lifts his hind leg under the night sky

A few rainbow Mobikes drive out of the abandoned lumber processing plant
drawing near from a distance, carrying on their backs a docile economy on the wing
After the rain the torrent in the river gains speed
leaving behind a shared rhythm and chemistry in vain

A fisherman takes out a search light from his vest and aims resolutely
Under the arch bridge, a startled white heron draws in an instant
a parabolic arc of urgency in the sky
His pregnant wife leans on the railing and gazes down

at the feast in the fish basket; barefooted children
holding toxic, sick fish in their hands vie to take pictures
On the triangular island, lovers steal kisses in the dark
The hurried tangling of limbs looks like a graceless tango

The night curtain is filthy and alarming
Raindrops wash the calcium-deficient city and its clustered buildings
A green-coated train touches the track exposed by earth
its rumbling plows open a tune of hidden rests

Translation by Michelle Yeh

Dozing at Middle Age

a side wind scratches the sun and sky
disturbing fifty-year-old dust

layered by thin air, even by fortune's
port window, I still hear your rasping cough

chin up, don't slouch
your wings expand with the sky, the feathers stir

in the distance, a whale, pregnant, not old but
frail too soon, the tenth month, no strength yet to bear

her labored journeys … fills this sky, deep as the sea
with smoke and nightmares.

Translation by Gregory Pardlo with Henry Zhang

Two Poems

CARPENTER'S UNIQUE DESIRE

Wood vanishes in the wood shavings.
Trees transform in the wood.
Forests disappear in trees.
Old Zhang's job is to make something
into something else,
turning geometry into an art.
For his whole life he has been making a chair
but he never sits. While standing, he has completed
the life of a craftsman
but never finished a chair.
When I was a boy
I was attracted to the sound he made with his saws.
I asked what he was making.
He said a chair that nobody could sit on.
I asked him when he would finish it. He said tomorrow.
It's tomorrow. I'm a grownup, with calluses on my butt.
But Old Zhang stands in the same place, among the shavings.
He takes root there, sprouting here and there.
Tapping and rapping. Some teeth are missing.
Is there such a thing as a chair that nobody can sit on?
I doubt it. But I'd rather believe it.
Some people are always on the move
like a speck of sawdust
looking for its previous life deep in the jungle.

Translation by Ming Di and Kerry Shawn Keys

WILDFLOWERS ON THE PLATEAU

I want, with *anyone*, to raise such beauties.
I want to move here and make the highlands
home. I want to live here, *here*, never cynical
about the world or wiping away my tears flowing
all day like mountain streams
from an unknown source—showing
how much I'm determined to grow old *here*,
here—to be their wild-haired old father.

Translation by Ming Di and Frank Stewart

Industrial Zone

The white light is on, the building is lit, the machine is on,
my fatigue is lit, the blueprint is lit...
It's Sunday night, the night of August 15,
the moonlight is on, a full hollow of emptiness, the lychee tree is lit,
a breeze blows the clear emptiness in its body while silence keeps
its year-round quietness, only insects sing in the bushes.
All the lights are on, the city is lit, so many dialects in the industrial
zone, so many humble people weak and homesick.
The industrial city. Sunday night.
The moonlight is on, the machine is lit, the blueprint is lit,
my face is lit—the rising moon lights up my falling heart.

Many lights are on, many people are passing by.
The lights in the industrial zone, my past my present the machine
the silent moonlight the silent lights the small me so small,
a piece of metal, a tool, a lamp—I warm up the industrial city
with my frail body. The bustling the noise the liveliness,
my tears my joy my pain,
my brilliant humble thoughts. My soul is lit
by the moonlight. It collects my thoughts and takes them to a faraway
place. They diminish and disappear in the light, unnoticed.

Translation by Ming Di

Wandering Wall, Tivoli Hotel,
Biloxi, MS, 2005.
Photograph by Linda Butler.

This beautiful old hotel had been closed
before Hurricane Katrina hit Biloxi. The
storm snapped the mooring cables of a
barge, which demolished this wall.

Remembrances and Gate,
Ocean Springs, MS, 2005.
Photograph by Linda Butler.

These crosses bear the names of family
members who died when their house
collapsed the first night of Katrina.
The family next door felt their house
shaking, escaped to the roof, and sur-
vived by tying themselves to a tree.

ZHOU QINGRONG

The History of China in Numbers

Five thousand years, two thousand years of legends, three thousand years of records.

Ten thousand harvests—how many people and animals did they feed? On 18,025,000 dawns the roosters crowed—to whom did dogs bark for 20,000 seasons?

One thousand years of wars of secession, a thousand years of wars of union, and a thousand years of fragmenting confederation. Two thousand years of reluctant fealty to temples, waving different flags, chanting different scriptures. Given one thousand years of true unity, five hundred would be taken by black nights. In the remaining five hundred years of brilliant days, how many hearts were scarred by unrecorded rainy days?

How many mysterious archives were sealed up by five hundred years of black nights? How many heroes were buried in earth? How many monuments were built by time for them? And where are the monuments? Sunshine tears through the clouds—how many monuments fall outside the territory of 9,600,000 square kilometers?

What I also want to calculate is: in these five thousand years how many days were earmarked for dreaming, how many days for justice and joy?

The numbers are certain. Five thousand years of endurance, five thousand years of living, five thousand for the great and the mean, and five thousand years of hope.

Love for five thousand years and loathing for five thousand years. Helpless love of this land for five thousand years. Violence, suffering, vile people achieving vast ambitions I refuse to count. The human heart is greater than five thousand years.

Translation by Michelle Chihara, Tony Barnstone, and Jia Yan

*Church Music, St. Michael Catholic
Church, Biloxi, MS, 2005.
Photograph by Linda Butler.*

*St. Michael Church was known for its
circular sanctuary and colorful stained-
glass windows. Katrina shattered the win-
dows; broken organ pipes and a hymnal lay
on the floor. Thanks to generous donations,
the church was fully restored by 2011.*

ZHU YU

Three Poems _____

EARLY AUTUMN IN ZHABEI

*Translator's Note: Zhabei is a district in Shanghai that saw great industri-
alization and cultural development in the early twentieth century, before
conflicts with invading Japanese forces in 1937. After capitalist reforms in
the 1980s, it was the formerly colonized areas of Shanghai—the "conces-
sions"—which began to flourish while Zhabei was, to a certain extent, left
behind. Hongkou, Baoshan, and Putuo are neighboring districts, and the
Suzhou River flows through Shanghai to the East China Sea.*

The trees' leaves fall, the trash cans are smeared
with the spotless tips of hybrid planes; soon
the tender greens and yellows will give way to umber.
No one's noticed, but now is its most solemn hour.

Emerging from Yonghe Road is Gonghe New Road. The asphalt surface
is enclosed within the limp light of the afternoon. This is
Shanghai Zhabei district; a hundred years past it filled out on the
    branch
then in the midst of war wilted quickly away.
Today, line one of the subway passes through its atrophied bulk,
it bursts out and brings to the surface a touch of autumn.

This touch of autumn has wind, not the kind that shakes leaves
    from their trees,
but the kind that seems to come from the ventilator factory
    on the corner.
This semi-derelict factory has the iron windows of an older time;
little glass is intact. The iron door still stands solid;
ivy creeps out from its cracks—

This autumn wind has touch, piercing the dense vine,
piercing the gray and mug of the everyday. In Zhabei
you mustn't think of neighboring Hongkou, Baoshan, or Putuo,
and don't look to the South, that the Suzhou River might bring,
aside from the crisp rebuke of autumn wind, the softness of water.

179

SCENE OF SUMMER

On the Yangtze's south bank, afternoon idly
slouches forth. This is an aesthetic space, its depths
stare down your gaze, its schemes of annexation,
once conquered, simpler, more complete—
On the narrow balcony, a clothes rack waves
the national flags of the quotidian:
discharged from sweat stains, finding
cheery cover in the scent of soap.
Let them move themselves in the windless air, to feign
inclusion in the human world. And let us take
a trip downstairs, from the eleventh floor to ground,
a right turn to the compound's doors which never close;
a journey through the crowds at the corner of Miyun Street.
Never have we been so close to the city's noise,
fulfilled and ripe, ignoring
a plain outsider listening in.
Dust coats the drooping leaves;
each knows its place along the branch, like the hidden order
which sets the stars upon the sky.
They thus survey those flimsy things which rise up
in the wind and rain and make you forget
all you know about botany and horticulture.
But wait. There is oleander,
the toxic flower,
its inviting reddened lip.

FRAGRANT GLADIOLUS

The night bobs slowly. After the series of events are in place
our feast will begin, everything will become bright.
I do not truly understand this kind of plant. The moment it blooms
it dazzles. I fear I will take myself for china and shatter.

The stories are simply too cold; it can be difficult for far-flung practices
    to take root,
fantasy gets blocked at the door, I can only come at it from the rituals
    of harvest:
With the first days of summer, the stigma extends from the leaves, bears
    flowers.
Six shallow rifts emerge, to form a tall bucket corolla, its body slight like
    gladiolus.
I cannot resist this kind of diversion, like I cannot refuse an invitation
    to drink.

Right now summer is distant, our colors still flat,
you and I can still note down the things that we said,
let the Chinese character wane in this plant's many names.
The secret has been planted beyond the reach of its scent, the military
    seal of a battle in progress.
In the depths of the thicket, let us ambush this season's insurrectionary
    forces.

Translations by Stephen Nashef

About the Photographer

LINDA BUTLER

Linda Butler's photographs have been exhibited widely, including at the Whitney Museum of American Art, Royal Ontario Museum in Toronto, and Yokohama Museum of Art in Japan. Her work has been collected by numerous museums, including the Boston Museum of Fine Arts, Cleveland Museum of Art, and San Francisco Museum of Modern Art. Her books include *Inner Light: The Shaker Legacy* (1985), *Rural Japan: Radiance of the Ordinary* (1992), *Italy: In the Shadow of Time* (1998), and *Yangtze Remembered: The River Beneath the Lake* (2004).

Republic of Apples, Democracy of Oranges contains work from two of Butler's portfolios that document momentous events, one caused by man and the other not.

YANGTZE REMEMBERED

The Yangtze River is the third longest river in the world. It originates in the high plateaus of Tibet, in southwestern China, and empties into the East China Sea 3,950 miles downstream. The city of Shanghai is built on a delta at its mouth. Between 2000 and 2003, Butler made seven trips to China to photograph the transformation of the Yangtze River Valley while the Three Gorges Dam was under construction. In 2003, with the dam's completion, the reservoir behind the dam began to form. It would eventually inundate 350 miles of the river valley, submerging 1,500 cities, towns, and villages, and displacing 1.3 million people. Butler writes:

> In 2000, on my first trip to the Yangtze River, the Three Gorges Dam Project was in an early stage. I was amazed by the immensity of the project. The old villages were still intact, but soon the government began building super highways on each side of the future reservoir as well as bridges to span it, and massive structures to prevent erosion. I made a total of seven trips over a three-year period. Much of what I photographed and published in the book *Yangtze Remembered: The River Beneath the Lake* is now gone forever.

KATRINA

Hurricane Katrina made landfall near Biloxi, Mississippi, on the morning of August 29, 2005. During that morning, storm surges as high as twenty-eight feet swept over the land, uprooting trees, killing hundreds of people, and forever changing the coast. The winds continued for days, spawning sixty-two tornadoes. The damage was so severe that people came from all over the country to help rebuild. In addition to FEMA staffers and electrical crews, church groups and college students volunteered to assist. A crew from California completely rebuilt a Buddhist temple. Butler writes:

> I was one of the photographers who felt "called" to create a record so that Americans would never forget this storm. On my first trip in October 2005, I found no accommodations and little fuel or food to buy. Without electricity, at sunset Mississippi's coastal towns became completely dark. It was so spooky that I decided to drive forty miles east to the house of a friend in Mobile, Alabama, which had food in the refrigerator, lights, and a warm bath.
>
> In the foggy Mississippi mornings that followed, a surreal landscape began to emerge. Sailboats with their masts askew were sitting in the middle of farmland, miles from the ocean. The storm carried pianos, beds, broken plates, and sofas into back yards. The homes that were still standing tilted away from the ocean; mold covered their interior walls.
>
> During the fourteen years since I created these images, other severe storms have had frightening effects. No one can definitively say which of these are "just weather" and which can be attributed to climate change. But if the past is any indication of the future, we can expect increasingly destructive storms as carbon dioxide and methane trap heat in the atmosphere.

For more of Linda Butler's work, see www.lindabutlerphoto.com.

About the Contributors

Aku Wuwu 阿库乌雾 is a Yi-Nuosu poet who writes in both Nuosu and Chinese. His books *Winter River* (1994) and *Tiger Traces* (1998) are the first collections of poetry written and published in modern Yi script and English. He is a professor of Yi Studies at Southwest University for Ethnic Nationalities, in Chengdu.

Sandra Alcosser is the author of *Except by Nature* (1998) and *A Fish to Feed All Hunger* (1993), honored by the National Poetry Series and the Larry Levis and William Stafford poetry awards. She was the NEA's first Conservation Poet for the Wildlife Conservation Society and Poets House, and Montana's first poet laureate.

Amang 阿芒 was born and raised in Hualien, Taiwan. Her books of poetry in translation are *On/Off: Selected Poems of Amang 1995–2002* (2003) and *No Daddy* (2008). She is a teacher in Taipei.

Baoyinhexige 宝音贺希格 is a poet and writer from Inner Mongolia who writes in Mongolian, Mandarin, and Japanese. His works include the Mongolian-language poetry collections *Another Kind of Moonlight* and *Ninety-Nine Black Mountain Goats*, and the Japanese-language prose work *I Am a Mongol*.

Trent Beauchamp-Sanchez is a social ecologist, antifascist, gardener, poet, and graduating senior at Whittier College.

Margo Berdeshevsky is the author of *Before The Drought* (2017), *Between Soul & Stone* (2011), *But a Passage in Wilderness* (2007), and *Beautiful Soon Enough* (2011), winner of the Ronald Sukenick Innovative Fiction Award. Her other honors include the Robert H. Winner Award from the Poetry Society of America. She lives and writes in Paris.

Bruce Bond is the author of twenty-one books, including *Rise and Fall of the Lesser Sun Gods* (2018), *Dear Reader* (2018) *Sacrum* (2017), *Blackout Starlight: New and Selected Poems 1997–2015* (2017), *Gold Bee* (2016), and *Black Anthem* (2016). He is a Regents Professor of English at University of North Texas.

Nickole Brown is the author of *Sister* (2018 revised edtion), *Fanny Says* (2015) and *To Those Who Were Our First Gods,* winner of the 2018 Rattle Chapbook Prize. She edits the Marie Alexander Poetry Series and teaches in the MFA Program at the Sewanee School of Letters. She lives with her wife, poet Jessica Jacobs, in North Carolina.

Elena Karina Byrne is the author of *Squander* (2016), *Masque* (2008), and *The Flammable Bird* (2002). She is the former Regional Director of the Poetry Society of America, Poetry Consultant/Moderator for *The Los Angeles Times* Festival of Books, and Literary Programs Director for The Ruskin Art Club.

Chen Dongdong 陈东东 was born in Shanghai in 1961. He graduated from Shanghai Normal University and began writing poetry in 1981. His recent publications include *Unbanned Title* (2011) and *The Guide Map* (2013). He lives in Shenzhen.

Chen He 沉河 was born in Qianjiang, Hubei province, and is a poet, essayist, and literary editor. In 2001, he joined the Yangtze River Art & Literature Publishing House, where he has edited the 21st Century Poetry Series and the *New Poetry Canon* (2013).

Chen Xianfa 陈先发 was born in 1967 in Anhui and graduated from Fudan University in Shanghai. His books of poetry include *The Problem of Raising Cranes* (2015) and *Crevice and Insight* (2016). He has also published the novel *Soul-Stealing Opera* (2006).

Dou Fengxiao 窦凤晓 was born in 1974 in Juxian, Shandong province, and now lives in Rizhao. Her works include *Testimony at the Edge of the Sky, In the Mountains,* and *By the Sea*. She is a member of the China Association for Promoting Democracy.

Duo Duo 多多 is the pen name of Li Shizheng. He was born in Beijing in 1951 and started writing poetry in the early 1970s. His books in translation include *The Boy Who Catches Wasps* (2002) and *Snow Plain* (2010). He is the first Chinese recipient of the Neustadt International Prize for Literature.

Natalie Fenaroli graduated from Whittier College in business and administration. A champion racecar driver, she currently works as a technical official for IndyCar, the sanctioning body for the premier-level open-wheel auto racing series in America.

Forrest Gander is the author of *Be With* (2018); *Eiko & Koma* (2013); *Core Samples from the World* (2011), a finalist for the 2012 Pulitzer Prize; *Eye*; and *Against Eye* (2005). His honors include a Whiting Award, two Gertrude Stein Awards for Innovative North American Writing, and fellowships from the NEA and Yaddo. He was elected a chancellor of the Academy of American Poets in 2017.

Gao Xing 高兴 was born in Jiangsu province in 1963 and graduated from Beijing Foreign Studies University. In addition to writing poems and essays, he has translated Milan Kundera, Ismail Kadare, Tomaz Salamun, and others into Chinese. He is the deputy editor-in-chief of the Chinese journal *World Literature*.

Vince Gotera is a professor of English at the University of Northern Iowa, where he served as editor of the *North American Review*. He now edits *Star*Line,* the journal of the Science Fiction and Fantasy Poetry Association. His books include Fighting Kite (2007) and the forthcoming *Pacific Crossing*. He blogs at *The Man with the Blue Guitar*.

Hai Zi 海子 (1964–1989) was raised in a farming village in Anhui province. At age twenty he began teaching at China University of Political Science and Law. Between 1984 and 1989, he wrote hundreds of poems. He committed suicide in 1989. A translation of his work in English, *Ripened Wheat,* was published in 2015.

Jane Hirshfield is the author of eight books, including *The Beauty*. Her honors include fellowships from the Guggenheim and Rockefeller foundations, the NEA, and the Academy of American Poets. A former chancellor of the Academy of American Poets, she has been poet-in-residence with the H.J. Andrews Experimental Forest and the neuroscience department of the University of California, San Francisco. In 2017, she founded Poets for Science.

Huang Bin 黄斌 was born in Chibi (Red Cliff), in southeastern Hubei province, in 1968. He won first place in the national poetry competition in 1994. His other honors include the ninth Qu Yuan Literary and Art Award. He studied journalism at Wuhan University and now works for the *Hubei Daily*.

Huang Lihai 黄礼孩 was born in Xuwen and now lives in Guangzhou. His books of poetry include *I Know Little about Life* and *The Passionate Mazurka*. He has also published books on art, dance, and film. His honors include the Lu Xun Literary Award of Guangdong province (2009) and Lebanon International Literary Award (2013).

Mark Irwin is the author of nine collections of poetry, including *A Passion According to Green* (2017), *American Urn: Selected Poems 1987–2014* (2015), *Tall If* (2008), and *Bright Hunger* (2004). His collection of essays, *Monster: Distortion, Abstraction, and Originality in Contemporary American Poetry*, appeared in 2017. He is a professor in the creative writing and literature program at the University of Southern California.

Jessica Jacobs is the author of *Pelvis with Distance* (2015), a biography-in-poems of the artist Georgia O'Keeffe, which won the New Mexico Book Award and was a finalist for the Lambda Literary Award. Her second collection is *Take Me with You, Wherever You're Going* (2019). She is associate editor for *Beloit Poetry Journal* and lives in North Carolina with her wife, poet Nickole Brown.

Jiang Hao 蒋浩 was born in Sichuan province in 1971. His books include a volume of essays and four poetry collections. His first book, *Rhetorics* (2005), won the Tendency Literature Award that year. He lives on Hainan Island.

Jiang Tao 姜涛 was born in Tianjin in 1970. His first book of poetry, *Bird Sutras,* won the Liu Li'an Prize for Poetry in 1997. His other books include *Four Poems* and *Mourning for Sometimes*. He is the editor of *An Anthology of New Verse and the Rise of Modern Poetry in China* (2005). He teaches Chinese literature at Beijing University in Beijing.

Jidi Majia 吉狄马加 is a Yi-Nuosu poet, born in Liangshan Yi Autonomous Prefecture in 1961. He came to national attention when his book *Song of My First Love* won the Third China National Poetry Prize, in 1988. His work has been translated into over twenty languages and published in over thirty countries. His most recent international awards include the Bucharest Poetry Prize (2017) and the Ianicius Prize of Poland (2017).

Jike Bu 吉克·布 (Jike Ayibujin) was born and grew up in Xichang, Yi Autonomous Prefecture of Sichuan province, in 1986. She was the first Yi woman awarded a master's degree in art. She began publishing poems while in college and has become known as one of the best Yi poets of the younger generation.

Ilyse Kusnetz (1966–2016) was a poet, essayist, journalist, and author of *Angel Bones* (2019); *Small Hours* (2014), winner of the T.S. Eliot Prize for Poetry; and *The Gravity of Falling* (2006). Her lyrics and voice are featured on The Interplanetary Acoustic Team's debut album *11 11 (Me, Smiling)*. A professor at Valencia College, she lived with her husband, poet Brian Turner, in Florida.

Ha Jin is a Chinese American poet and novelist. He was born in Jinzhou, Liaoning province, in 1956 and emigrated to the U.S. following the Tiananmen Square incident in 1989. He has published seven books of poetry and eight novels, among other books. His honors include the National Book Award for Fiction and PEN/Faulkner and PEN/Hemingway Awards. He was a finalist for the Pulitzer Prize in 2005.

Lei Pingyang 雷平阳 was born in Yunnan province in 1966. His book of poetry *Notes on Yunnan* won the Lu Xun Award. His other works include *Montages in the Wind* and *Notes on Pu'er Tea*. He teaches at the Yunnan Normal University.

Li Heng 黎衡 was born in Shiyan, Hubei province, in 1986. His awards include the Liu Li-an Poetry Prize, the Weiming Poetry Prize, the *China Times* Literary Award, and the DJS–Poetry East West Award. He works as a journalist in Guangzhou.

Li Hongwei 李宏伟 was born in Jiangyou, Sichuan province, in 1978. He won the 2014 Young Writers Annual Performance Award and the Xu Zhimo Award. His books of poetry include *10 Kinds of Imagination in Contemporary Life*. He has written two novels and the story collection *Fake Time Party*. He lives in Beijing.

Li Nan 李南 was born in 1952. He is a painter as well as a poet. His books include *Meeting of the Swords* (1977) and *In Memory of My Mother* (1978).

Li Sen 李森 was born in Yunna in 1966, where he continues to reside. His works include *Shadows on the Canvas* (2000), *Accounts of Animals* (2002), and *Cangshan Night Talk* (2006). He teaches at Yunnan University.

Li Shaojun 李少君 was born in 1967 in Hunan, central China. He lived in Hainan province (South Sea Island) for twenty-five years, working as editor of the journal *Tianya*. His poetry collections include *Grassroots* (2010), *Nature* (2014), and *A Small Station Where God Arrives* (2016). He is the associate chief editor of *Poetry Monthly* in Beijing.

Li Suo 里所 was born in Xinjiang Uyghur Autonomous Region and lives and works in Beijing. She is a poet, translator, and editor at Xiron Publishing. She holds degrees from Xi'an International Studies University and Beijing Normal University.

Shirley Geok-lin Lim is professor emerita at University of California, Santa Barbara, where she was awarded the Multiethnic Literatures of the United States Lifetime Achievement Award. Her first book, *Crossing the Peninsula* (1980), received the Commonwealth Poetry Prize, and was followed by seven poetry collections, three short-story collections, two adult novels, a children's novel, and *The Shirley Lim Collection* (2013). Her memoir, *Among the White Moon Faces* (1996), received the American Book Award.

Ling Yu 零雨 was born in Taiwan and has published four books of poetry. She received her master's degree from the University of Wisconsin, Madison. She resides in Taipei and Yilan and teaches at National Yilan Institute of Technology.

Lü De'an 吕德安 is a poet and painter. His books of poetry include *Paper Snake, The Other Half of Life, The South to the North, Obstinate Stones,* and *Right Where One Belongs*. In 2011 he won the Yunnan Gaoligong Poetry Prize, and established Fujian's Friday Painting Society. He lives in Beijing, where he devotes his time to painting.

Sarah Maclay is the author of three books of poetry: *Music for the Black Room* (2011), *The White Bride* (2008), and *Whore* (2004). She teaches at Loyola Marymount University, in California.

David Mason is the author of many collections of poetry and prose. His latest books are *Voices, Places: Essays* (2018) and *The Sound: New and Selected Poems* (2018). From 2010 to 2014 he served as poet laureate of Colorado.

Mo Fei 莫非 was born in 1960 and is a poet, photographer, and naturalist. Among his poetry collections are *The Hollow Emptiness, Words and Things,* and *Selected Short Poems.* His prose includes *Datura Manuscripts, A Brief on Economy,* and the poetic drama *Orchestra of Madmen.*

Mo Mo 默默 was born in 1964. In 1985 he co-founded the poetry school Sa Jiao (撒娇派), which he says means "gentle resistance," and its journal. He was jailed in 1986 for his long poem "Growing Up in China." He now runs a residence in Shanghai for wandering poets.

Stanley Moss was born in New York State in 1925. His books of poetry include *It's About Time* (2015), *God Breaketh Not All Men's Hearts Alike: New & Later Collected Poems* (2011), *Rejoicing: New and Collected Poems* (2009), *New & Selected Poems: 2006* (2006), and *Songs of Imperfection* (2005).

Mushasijia Eni (Li Hui) 俄尼·牧莎斯加 (李慧) is a member of the Yi ethnic group and is from Jiulong, Sichuan province. He has been a member of the China Writers' Association since 2005, and his works include *The Soul Has a Date, The Tribe and the Lover,* and *Highland Potatoes,* as well as the script for the television series *Zhige'a'er.*

Na Ye 娜夜 is an ethnic Manchu poet. Her family was from Niaoning province, northeast China, but she grew up in western China. After graduating from Nanjing University, she became a journalist in Lanzhou city, Gansu province.

Naomi Shihab Nye is the author of many books of poems, including *Transfer* (2011); *You and Yours* (2005), which received the Isabella Gardner Poetry Award; and *19 Varieties of Gazelle: Poems of the Middle East* (2002). She has been a Lannan, Guggenheim, and Witter Bynner Fellow. She served as a chancellor of the Academy of American Poets from 2010 to 2015.

Pan Xichen 潘洗尘 was born in 1964 in Heilongjiang, northeastern China. He founded *Poetry EMS Weekly* in 2009 and started *Reading Poetry* quarterly in 2010. He resides in Dali, Yunnan, and in his hometown in Heilongjiang.

Alan Michael Parker is the author of nine books, including *The Ladder* (2016). He is the Houchens Professor of English at Davidson College and also teaches in the University of Tampa's low-residency MFA program. He lives in North Carolina.

Kevin Prufer is the author of seven poetry collections, most recently *How He Loved Them* (2018), *Churches* (2014), and *In a Beautiful Country* (2011). The recipient of grants from the Lannan Foundation and the NEA, he is a professor in the creative writing program at the University of Houston.

Qiu Huadong 邱华栋 was born in Xinjiang Uyghur Autonomous Region, in northwest China, in 1969. His books include *The Starlight in Hands* (2016) and *Gold Fantasy*

(2017). He is the associate director of the Lu Xun Literary Institute in Beijing and the associate editor-in-chief of *People's Literature* magazine.

Suzanne Roberts holds degrees in biology and English, and a doctorate in literature and the environment. Her books of poetry include *Plotting Temporality* (2012), *Three Hours to Burn a Body: Poems on Travel* (2011), *Nothing to You* (2008), and *Shameless* (2007). She is also author of *Almost Somewhere: Twenty-Eight Days on the John Muir Trail* (2012).

Brianna Lyn Sahagian-Limas is a writer, educator, and library professional from southern California. She has published poetry and fiction in *Greenleaf Review* and *River's Voice*.

Nicholas Samaras is from Patmos, Greece. His books of poetry include *American Psalm, World Psalm* (2014) and *Hands of the Saddlemaker* (1992), winner of the Yale Series of Younger Poets Award. His work has been published in *The New Yorker, Poetry, The New York Times, New Republic, Kenyon Review,* and elsewhere.

Shen Haobo 沈浩波 was born in Jiangsu province in 1976. He is a major advocate of the Lower Body poetry movement, which attempts to overcome the taboos against explicit content in poetry. His first poetry collection, *Great Evil in the Heart* (2004), was banned. His most recent collection is *Command Me to Be Silent.* He is the founder of Xiron, a successful independent publishing house in Beijing.

Shen Wei 沈苇 was born in 1965 in Huzhou, Zhejiang province, and moved to Xinjiang Uyghur Autonomous Region, in western China, in 1988. A teacher, journalist, and now editor-in-chief of the regional literary magazine *The West,* he has published seven books of poetry. He won the first Lu Xun Literature Award in 1998.

John Shoptaw is the author of *Times Beach* (2015), winner of the Northern California Poetry Prize, concerning the Mississippi River watershed. He teaches poetry at the University of California, Berkeley.

Song Wei 宋炜 was born in 1964 in Sichuan province. A hermit, he has received many friendly offers for publication, but has not yet published a book of poetry.

Gerald Stern was born in Pittsburgh in 1925. His most recent books of poetry include *Galaxy Love* (2017), *Divine Nothingness* (2014), *In Beauty Bright* (2012), *Early Collected Poems: 1965–1992* (2010), and *Save the Last Dance* (2008). Among other honors, he served as a chancellor of the Academy of American Poets in 2006.

Sun Wenbo 孙文波 was born in Sichuan province and lives in Shenzhen. He was a factory worker and a soldier before becoming a literary editor in the mid-1980s. He launched the magazine *The Nineties,* with Xiao Kaiyu, in 1989, and was the chief editor of *Contemporary Poetry.*

Terese Svoboda is a poet, novelist, essayist, biographer, and translator. Her recent poetry collections include *Professor Harriman's Steam Air-Ship* (2016) and *When the Next Big War Blows Down the Valley: Selected and New Poems* (2015). She is the recipient of the Cecil Hemley Award, the Emily Dickinson Prize, the Iowa Poetry Prize, and fellowships from the Guggenheim Foundation and the New York Foundation for the Arts.

Chad Sweeney is the author of six collections of poetry, including *Little Million Doors* (2019), and two books of translation (Farsi and Spanish). His poems have appeared in *Best American Poetry*, *The Pushcart Prize Anthology*, *New American Writing*, and elsewhere. He is an associate professor of creative writing at California State University, San Bernardino, where he edits *Ghost Town Literary Journal*.

Arthur Sze is the recipient of the Jackson Poetry Prize from *Poets & Writers* and was recently elected a fellow of the American Academy of Arts & Sciences. His tenth book of poetry is *Sight Lines* (2019).

Tashi Tentso 扎西旦措 is a Tibetan poet born in the 1970s. As with most minority women poets in China, very little is known about her.

Daniel Tobin is the author of eight books of poems, including *Blood Labors* (2018) and *From Nothing* (2016), and a book of versions from the German of Paul Celan, *The Stone in the Air* (2018). His honors include the Massachusetts Book Award, the Julia Ward Howe Award, the Stephen Meringoff Award, and fellowships from the NEA and Guggenheim Foundation.

Un Sio San 袁紹珊 was born in Macau. She has won numerous awards, including the Luce Foundation fellowships and the Macau Literature Prize. Her poetry collections include *Here* (2011), *Exile in the Blossom Time* (2008), and *Wonderland* (2001). Her latest essay collection is *Boisterous Islands*.

Wang Jiaxin 王家新 was born in Danjiangkou, Hubei province, in 1957. His first collection of poems in English is *Darkening Mirror: New and Selected Poems* (2016). He is currently a professor of literature at Renmin University in Beijing.

Wang Ping was born in Shanghai in 1957. Her books of poetry include *Ten Thousand Waves* (2014) and *The Magic Whip* (2003). Her nonfiction book *Aching for Beauty: Footbinding in China* (2000) won the Eugene Kayden Award; and her short-story collection, *The Last Communist Virgin* (2007), won the 2008 Minnesota Book Award. She is the founder of the Kinship of Rivers Project, which brings together the communities along the Yangtze and Mississippi rivers through the arts.

Wang Yin 王寅 was born in 1962 in Shanghai and is a poet, photographer, and journalist. His publications include: *Selected Poems of Wang Yin*, and *Art Is Not the Only Way* (interviews with artists). His book *Limelight* won the Jiangnan and Dong Dang Zi poetry awards. He lives and works in Shanghai.

Charles Harper Webb is the author of, most recently, *Sidebend World* (2018), *A Million MFAs Are Not Enough* (2016), and *What Things Are Made Of* (2013). He is the recipient of grants from the Whiting and Guggenheim foundations, and teaches creative writing at California State University, Long Beach.

Jonathan Weinert is the author, most recently, of *Thirteen Small Apostrophes* (2013) and *In the Mode of Disappearance* (2008), winner of the Nightboat Poetry Prize. He is co-editor, with Kevin Prufer, of *Until Everything Is Continuous Again: American Poets on the Recent Work of W. S. Merwin* (2014). He lives in Massachusetts.

William Wenthe has published four books of poems, including *God's Foolishness* (2016) and *Words Before Dawn* (2012). He has received poetry fellowships from the NEA and the Texas Commission on the Arts. Originally from northern New Jersey, he teaches at Texas Tech University.

Xi Du 西渡 was born in Zhejiang province in 1967. He graduated from Beijing University in 1989. After working as an editor, he went to Qinghua University for a doctorate in Chinese literature, where he teaches. His works include four books of poetry and three collections of critical reviews.

Xiao Shui 肖水 was born in Chenzhou, Hunan province, in 1980. He has a degree in law and Chinese literature from Fudan University. He lives and works in Shanghai. His books include *Lost and Found, Chinese Class,* and *Chinese Mugwort: New Jueju Poetry.*

Xu Lizhi 许立志 (1990–2014) was born in rural Jieyang, in Guangdong province. A migrant laborer, he produced many poems while working on an assembly line at Foxconn, in Shenzhen. He committed suicide at the factory at age twenty-four. His death as well as his poems became headline news nationally and internationally. His poems can be found online and in several anthologies.

Yang Jian 杨健 was born in Anhui province in 1967. His books include *Ancient Bridge* (2007) and *Remorse* (2009). His honors include the Liu Li'an Poetry Award, Rougang Poetry Prize, Yulong Poetry Prize, and the Chinese Literature Media Award.

Yang Ke 杨克 was born in 1957 in Guangxi province. He has published eleven books of poetry. His honors include the Lu Xun Literary Prize for Guangdong province and the Chinese Contemporary Poetry Distinguished Achievement Award (2000–2010). He is the deputy chairman of the Guangdong Writers' Association. His translations into English include *Two Halves of the World Apple* (2017).

Yang Mu 杨牧 was born in Taiwan in 1940. His over sixty books of poetry and prose include *Hawk of the Mind: Collected Poems* (2015) and *Memories of Mount Qilai: The Education of a Young Poet* (2015). He has received the Newman Prize for Chinese Literature and the Cikada Prize (Sweden). He is professor emeritus at the University of Washington, Seattle; distinguished professor at National Normal University, Taipei; and distinguished professor emeritus at Dong Hwa University, Hualien, Taiwan.

Yang Senjun 杨森君 is from the Ningxia Hui Autonomous Region, predominantly inhabited by Chinese Muslims. He was born in 1962 in Lingwu, Ningxia province, and became nationally known in 2005, when he won the Rougang Poetry Award.

Yao Feng 姚风 was born in Beijing in 1958 and is now a professor at the University of Macau. His books of poetry include *Writing on the Wings of the Wind, One Horizon—Two Views, Faraway Song,* and *When the Fish Close Their Eyes.* He received the Rougang Poetry Award in 2004.

Yu Xiaozhong 余笑忠 was born in the rural area of Qichun County, in eastern Hubei province, in 1965. He graduated from Beijing Broadcasting Institute in 1986 and has worked for Hubei TV since then. He won the 2003 Chinese Poetry Prize awarded jointly by the *Star Poetry Monthly* and *Poetry Monthly,* the third Yangtze River Poetry Prize, and the twelfth October Literary Prize in 2015.

Yu Xiuhua 余秀华 was born with cerebral palsy in rural Hengdian village in Hubei province. She became well known in 2014, when she posted three lines of her poem "Crossing Half of China to Sleep with You" on her blog. Encouraged by a top editor, she published books of poems in 2015 that became bestsellers.

Zang Di 臧棣 was born in Beijing in 1964. He serves on *Modern Poetry Review*'s editorial board and edits the *Chinese Poetry Review*. His books of poetry include *Chronicles of Swallow Garden, Disturbances,* and *Fresh Brambles*. His honors include the River International Poetry Festival, Yangtze Literary Arts, and Su Manshu Poetry Awards.

Matthew Zapruder is the author of *Why Poetry* (2017), a book of prose, and the poetry collections *Sun Bear* (2014), *Come on All You Ghosts* (2010), and *The Pajamaist* (2006), among other works. His honors include the May Sarton poetry award from the American Academy of Arts and Sciences; the William Carlos Williams Award from the Poetry Society of America; and Lannan and Guggenheim fellowships.

Zhai Yongming 翟永明 was born in Chengdu, Sichuan province, in 1955, and is one of the best known feminist poets in China. She has several collections of poems and essays. Among her honors is the Zhongkun Poetry Award. She lives in Beijing and Chengdu.

Zhang Er 张尔 was born in 1976 in Anhui province and is the chief editor of *Enclave*, a journal founded in 2012 in Shenzhen that publishes poetry, literary criticism, philosophy, and art. His poetry has been translated into English, French, and Swedish.

Zhang Qinghua 张清华 is the executive director of the International Writing Center at Beijing Normal University. His honors include the 2010 Critics Award of the annual Chinese Literature Awards from the Southern Media Group. His books include the anthologies *Thirty Years of Avant-garde Poetry in China 1979–2009* and *Mapping the Independent Poetry in China*.

Zhang Zhihao 张执浩 is a poet and novelist. Born in 1965 in Jingmen, Hubei province, he has published five novels and four collections of poetry. He won the Poetry of the Year Award (2002), the People's Literature Award (2004), the October Prize (2014), and the gold prize of the first China Qu Yuan Poetry Prize (2014).

Zheng Xiaoqiong 郑小琼 was born in Sichuan province in 1980. She moved to Dongguan city in southern Guangdong province as a migrant worker in 2001 and wrote poetry during the six years she worked in a hardware factory. She won the Liqun Literature Award from *People's Literature* (2007) and is now an editor in Guangdong.

Zhou Qingrong 周庆荣 was born in Xiangshui, Jiangsu province, in 1963 and now lives in Beijing. His recent collections include *Selected Prose Poems of Zhou Qingrong* (2006), *We* (bilingual edition, 2010), *People with Lofty Ideals* (2011), *Prediction* (2014), and *People with a Vision* (2014).

Zhu Yu 茱萸 is the pen name of Zhu Qinyun. His publications include *Prelude: The Spirit of Flowers, Cadence by the Furnace, The Flow and Fruit of Poetry,* and *The Feast and Its Invitation*. His work has been translated into English, Japanese, Russian, and French. He teaches at Suzhou University in Jiangsu province.

TRANSLATORS

Neil Aitken holds a doctorate from the University of Southern California. His first book of poetry, *The Lost Country of Sight* (2008), won the Philip Levine Prize; his most recent book of poetry is *Babbage's Dream* (2017). He co-translated with Ming Di *The*

Book of Cranes: Selected Poems of Zang Di (2015) and has contributed to *New Cathay: Contemporary Chinese Poetry* (2013). He received the DJS Translation Prize in 2011.

Mark Bender is professor in Chinese and chair of the department of East Asian Languages and Literature at Ohio State University. His most recent book is *The Borderlands of Asia: Culture, Place, Poetry,* which features poems by forty-eight poets in North East India, Myanmar, Southwest China, Inner Mongolia, and Mongolia (2017).

Steve Bradbury taught English literature in Taiwan for many years, and now lives in Florida. His books of translation include *Poems from the Prison Diary of Ho Chi Minh* (2003) and *Feelings Above Sea Level: Prose Poems from the Chinese of Shang Qin* (2006). His translation of Hsia Yu's *Salsa* (2014) was shortlisted for the Lucien Stryk Prize.

Michelle Chihara received her doctorate from the University of California, Irvine, and now teaches at Whittier College. She has published in many places, including *Mother Jones, The Boston Phoenix,* and *The Los Angeles Review of Books.*

Alexandra Draggeim has studied in China, Paris, and elsewhere. She graduated from Ohio State University and is now a freelance writer and translator. Her working languages are English, Russian, Chinese, and French.

Du Xian 杜鲜 is an associate professor of the School of Literature, Yunnan University. His research is in ethnic cultures and arts, especially in the Buddhist arts of the Nanzhao and Dali kingdoms.

Fang Xia is a doctoral student in creative writing in the Department of English, University of Macau.

Rachel Galvin is the author of the poetry collections *Lost Property Unit* (2017) and *Pulleys & Locomotion* (2009). Her translations include Raymond Queneau's *Hitting the Streets* (2013), winner of the 2014 Scott Moncrieff Prize. She is an assistant professor at the University of Chicago.

Steven Haven is a professor of English and director of the MFA program in creative writing at Lesley University. His books include *The Last Sacred Place in North America* (poetry), *Dust and Bread* (poetry), *The River Lock* (memoir), and *The Long Silence of the Mohawk Carpet Smokestacks* (poetry). He was a Fulbright teaching fellow in Beijing.

Jia Yan was a visiting scholar of Chinese literature at the University of Oklahoma in 2018. Her publications include *The Journey of Chinese Contemporary Authors* and *An Overview of the Translation of Chinese Contemporary Poetry.*

Kit Kelen is an Australian poet and former professor of creative writing in the Department of English, University of Macau. He has co-translated two volumes with the late Hong Kong poet Leung Ping Kwan, and four with Macau poet Yao Jing Ming.

Kerry Shawn Keys has published nearly fifty books, including poetry, plays, fiction, and children's literature. He is the recipient of NEA and Poetry Society of America awards, and translation awards from the Lithuanian Writers' Union. A member of International PEN, he is the Republic of Užupis' World Poetry ambassador.

Li Yongyi 李永毅 is a professor of English at Chongquing University. His books include *Catullus' Carmina* (2008), *A Study of Catullus* (2009), *Selected Poems of Horace* (2015),

On the Art of Horace (2016), and *The Complete Poetry of Horace* (2017). He received the 2014–2017 Lu Xun Literature Prize for translation.

Liang Yujing grew up in China and is a doctoral candidate at Victoria University of Wellington, New Zealand. He is the Chinese translator of *Best New Zealand Poems 2014* and the English translator of *Zero Distance: New Poetry from China*.

Andrea Lingenfelter is the translator of *The Last Princess of Manchuria* (1992) and *Farewell My Concubine* (1993) by Li Pik-wah (Lilian Lee), and *Candy* by Mian Mian (2003). Her other translations include *The Changing Room: Selected Poetry of Zhai Yongming* (2012), winner of the Northern California Book Award, and *The Kite Family* (2005), a collection of Hon Lai Chu's surrealistic short fiction, for which he was awarded an NEA translation fellowship. She teaches at the University of San Francisco.

Denis Mair holds a master's degree in Chinese from Ohio State University and has taught at the University of Pennsylvania and Yunnan University. He has translated Yan Li, Mai Cheng, Meng Lang, Jidi Majia, and many other poets. His translation of art criticism by Zhu Zhu was published by Hunan Fine Arts Press in 2009.

Stephen Nashef was born in Glasgow, Scotland, and lives in Guangzhou, where he translates and writes. His translations have appeared in *Pathlight* and *Tender Buds: 21st Century Chinese Poems*, and he has written for the U.S. journal *Chinese Literature and Culture.* He is a founding editor of the UK poetry magazine *Kaffeeklatsch.*

Gregory Pardlo is the author of *Totem* (2007), winner of the APR/Honickman First Book Prize; and *Digest* (2014), winner of the Pulitzer Prize for Poetry. He was awarded a Guggenheim Fellowship in 2017. He is poetry editor for *Virginia Quarterly Review* and teaches in the MFA program at Rutgers University. He lives in Brooklyn.

Lawrence Smith is the author of eight books of poetry, a memoir, five books of fiction, two biographies (of Lawrence Ferlinghetti and Kenneth Patchen), and two books of translation of Chinese poetry. He is professor emeritus of Bowling Green State University's Firelands College, and director of the Firelands Writing Center and Bottom Dog Press. His recent books include *The Thick of Thin: Memoirs of Working Class Writers* (2017) and a new edition of *Thoreau's Lost Journal: Poems* (2018).

Frank Stewart is a recipient of the Whiting Writers Award. His edited books include *The Poem Behind the Poem: Translating Asian Poetry* (2004). His translations, with Michelle Yeh, are included in *Hawk of the Mind: Collected Poems of Yang Mu* (2018). He has also translated *I, Snow Leopard* by Jidi Majia (2016); other translations have appeared in *Chinese Poetry Today, World Literature Today,* and *Harvard Review On-line: "Omniglots."*

Jeremy Tiang has translated more than ten books from Chinese. He has been awarded a PEN/ Heim Grant, an NEA Literary Translation Fellowship, and a People's Literature Award Mao-Tai Cup. His short-story collection *It Never Rains on National Day* was shortlisted for the Singapore Literature Prize.

Denise Wong Velasco was raised in Hong Kong and is the administrative coordinator for the Luce Initiative on Asian Studies and the Environment at Whittier College

Wang Hao 王浩 teaches English at Yunnan University and devotes much of his time to translation. His books in translation include *Chinese Windmill* (2007), *The Third Pole* (2015), and *The Museum of Time* (2017).

Michelle Yeh is Distinguished Professor in the Department of East Asian Languages and Cultures at the University of California, Davis. She is the co-editor and co-translator of *No Trace of the Gardener: Poems of Yang Mu* (1998) and *Hawk of the Mind: Collected Poems of Yang Mu* (2018). Her other publications include *Modern Chinese Poetry: Theory and Practice Since 1917* (1991); *Anthology of Modern Chinese Poetry* (1994); and *Frontier Taiwan: An Anthology of Modern Chinese Poetry* (2014).

Henry Zhang 张晴 grew up in the U.S. and is a graduate student in the Department of Chinese Literature at Beijing Normal University. He participated in several international translation workshops at Beijing Normal University and is a recipient of the 2017 Henry Luce Translation Fellowship in the U.S.

GUEST EDITORS

Tony Barnstone is a professor of English and environmental studies at Whittier College. A prolific poet, author, essayist, and literary translator, he is the author of twenty books. His latest poetry book is *Pulp Sonnets* (2015). His books of co-translation include *Mother Is a Bird: Sonnets by a Yi Poet* (2017), *River Merchant's Wife* by Ming Di (2012), *Chinese Erotic Poems* (2007), *The Anchor Book of Chinese Poetry* (2005), and *Out of the Howling Storm: The New Chinese Poetry* (1993). Among his honors are fellowships from the NEA, the NEH, and the California Arts Council. He has won the Grand Prize of the Strokestown International Poetry Festival, the Pushcart Prize, the Pablo Neruda Prize, and the John Ciardi Prize.

Ming Di 明迪 is a Chinese poet based in the U.S. She attended Boston College and Boston University, where she taught Chinese. She has published six books of poetry in Chinese along with a collaborative translation, *River Merchant's Wife* (2012). She co-translated *The Book of Cranes* by Zang Di (2015) with Neil Aitken, and *Empty Chairs: Selected Poems* by Liu Xia (2015) with Jennifer Stern, which was a finalist for the 2016 Best Translation Book Award. She edited and co-translated *New Cathay: Contemporary Chinese Poetry* (2013) and *New Poetry from China 1917–2017* (2019). In 2013 and 2014, she received Henry Luce Foundation fellowships. A co-founder of *Poetry East West* journal, she serves as the China editor for *Poetry International Rotterdam*. She has also translates from English into Chinese, most recently *Observations* by Marianne Moore (2018).

Poets by Geographical Location

China South

Duo Duo 多多 (South Sea Island)
Huang Lihai 黄礼孩 (Guangdong)
Jiang Hao 蒋浩 (South Sea Island)
Li Heng 黎衡 (Guangdong)
Li Shaojun 李少君 (South Sea Island)
Sun Wenbo 孙文波 (Shenzhen)
Xu Lizhi 许立志 (Guangdong)
Yang Ke 杨克 (Guangdong)
Zhang Er 张尔 (Shenzhen)
Zheng Xiaoqiong 郑小琼 (Guangdong)

Taiwan and Macau

Amang 阿芒 (Taiwan)
Ling Yu 零雨 (Taiwan)
Un Sio San 袁紹珊 (Macau)
Yang Mu 杨牧 (Taiwan)
Yao Feng 姚风 (Macau)

Southwest

Aku Wuwu 阿库乌雾 (Sichuan)
Jidi Majia 吉狄马加 (Sichuan)
Jike Bu 吉克·布 (Sichuan)
Lei Pingyang 雷平阳 (Yunnan)
Li Sen 李森 (Yunnan)
Mo Fei 莫非 (Yunnan)
Mo Mo 默默 (Yunnan)
Mushasijia Eni (Li Hui) 俄尼·牧莎斯加 (李慧) (Sichuan)
Song Wei 宋炜 (Sichuan)

Central

Chen He 沉河 (Hubei)
Chen Xianfa 陈先发 (Anhui)
Huang Bin 黄斌 (Hubei)
Yang Jian 杨健 (Anhui)
Yu Xiuhua 余秀华 (Hubei)
Yu Xiaozhong 余笑忠 (Hubei)
Zhang Zhihao 张执浩 (Hubei)

West

Na Ye 娜夜 (Gansu)

Shen Wei 沈苇 (Xinjiang)

Tashi Tentso 扎西旦措 (Tibet)

Yang Senjun 杨森君 (Ningxia)

North

Baoyinhexige 宝音贺希格 (Inner Mongolia)

Gao Xing 高兴 (Beijing)

Hai Zi 海子 (Beijing)

Jiang Tao 姜涛 (Tianjin)

Li Hongwei 李宏伟 (Beijing)

Li Nan 李南 (Hebei)

Li Suo 里所 (Beijing)

Pan Xichen 潘洗尘 (Heilongjiang)

Qiu Huadong 邱华栋 (Beijing)

Shen Haobo 沈浩波 (Beijing)

Wang Jiaxin 王家新 (Beijing)

Xi Du 西渡 (Beijing)

Zang Di 臧棣 (Beijing)

Zhai Yongming 翟永明 (Beijing)

Zhou Qingrong 周庆荣 (Beijing)

East

Chen Dongdong 陈东东 (Shanghai)

Dou Fengxiao 窦凤晓 (Shandong)

Wang Yin 王寅 (Shanghai)

Xiao Shui 肖水 (Shanghai)

Zhang Qinghua 张清华 (Shandong)

Zhu Yu 茱萸 (Suzhou)

Southeast

Lü De'an 吕德安 (Fu Jian)

U.S. West

Sandra Alcosser (California)

Trent Beauchamp-Sanchez (California)

Elena Karina Byrne (California)

Jane Hirshfield (California)

Mark Irwin (California)

Shirley Geok-lin Lim (California)

Sarah Maclay (California)

David Mason (Colorado)

Suzanne Roberts (California)

Brianna Lyn Sahagian-Limas (California)

John Shoptaw (California)

Chad Sweeney (California)

Charles Harper Webb (California)
Matthew Zapruder (California)

Southwest
Bruce Bond (Texas)
Naomi Shihab Nye (Texas)
Kevin Prufer (Texas)
Arthur Sze (New Mexico)
William Wenthe (Texas)

Midwest
Vince Gotera (Iowa)
Wang Ping (Minnesota)

Southeast
Nickole Brown (North Carolina)
Jessica Jacobs (North Carolina)
Ilyse Kusnetz (Florida)
Alan Michael Parker (North Carolina)

Northeast
Ha Jin (Massachusetts)
Stanley Moss (New York)
Nicholas Samaras (New York)
Gerald Stern (New Jersey)
Terese Svoboda (New York)
Daniel Tobin (Massachusetts)
Jonathan Weinert (Massachusetts)

Expatriate
Margo Berdeshevsky (France)
Alicia Stallings (Greece)

Permissions

"Avenging Deer," "Red-fruited Hawthorn," and "Wolf Skin" by Aku Wuwu. From *Coyote Traces: Aku Wuwu's Poetic Sojourn in America,* translated by Wen Peihong and Mark Bender. Columbus, OH: Foreign Language Publications, 2015. Reprinted by permission of Ohio State University.

"Grass Effigy" by Aku Wuwu, translated by Mark Bender. From *Chinese Literature Today* 4:1 (2014). Copyright © University of Oklahoma, reprinted by permission of Taylor & Francis Ltd on behalf of University of Oklahoma.

"Crows" by Baoyinhexige, translated by Mark Bender. From *Chinese Literature Today* 4:1 (2014). Copyright © University of Oklahoma, reprinted by permission of Taylor & Francis Ltd on behalf of University of Oklahoma.

"Light Up" by Chen Dongdong, "Questions of Cranes" by Chen Xianfa, "Think of This Word" by Duo Duo, "A Small Town Where Rivers Run Backward" by Gu Ma, "Walking in the Woods" by Huang Bin, "Call Her Suoma" by Jike Bu, "Happy Ants" by Lei Pingyang, "Dreaming of a Tiger's Corpse" by Li Hongwei, "God Comes to a Small Bus Station" by Li Shaojun, "Some Floating Time in Light—For You" by Mo Fei, "Joy" by Na Ye, "Small Notes in My Old Age" by Song Wei, "Watching Crows in the Summer Palace" by Xi Du, "Food Is Running Out" by Xiao Shui, "I Swallow an Iron Moon" by Xu Lizhi, "Carpenter's Unique Desire" by Zhang Zhihao, and "Industrial Zone" by Zheng Xiaoqiong. From *New Poetry from China 1916–2017,* edited by Ming Di. NY: Black Square Editions, 2019. Reprinted by permission of the translators.

"Snow in Ulan Bator" by Jiang Tao. From *World Literature Today* 89:5 (2015) and *Ghost Fishing: An Eco-Justice Poetry Anthology,* edited by Melissa Tuckey. Athens, GA: University of Georgia Press, 2018. Reprinted by permission of the translator.

"A Sacred Mango" by Ha Jin. From *Between Silences: A Voice from China.* Chicago: University of Chicago Press, 1990. Reprinted by permission of the author.

"Orange in the Wilderness" by Li Sen. From *Feng: Poetry China.* Los Angeles: DJS Books, 2017. Reprinted by permission of the translator.

"Night at Ocean Corner, and Women" by Lü De'an. From *Gulf Coast* (winter/spring 2015). Reprinted by permission of the translator.

"An Embroidery Needle Made from a Water-Deer Fang" by Mushasijia Eni, translated by Alexandra Draggeim. From *Chinese Literature Today* 4:1 (2014). Copyright © University of Oklahoma, reprinted by permission of Taylor & Francis Ltd on behalf of University of Oklahoma.

"Carpenter" and "A Taoist Priest on Mount Kongtong" by Shen Haobo. From *Puerto del Sol* (September 2017). Reprinted by permission of the translator.

"Bland Life, Blunt Poetry" and "Nothing to Do with Crows" by Sun Wenbo. From *New Cathay: Contemporary Chinese Poetry*, edited by Ming Di. North Adams, MA: Tupelo Press, 2013. Reprinted by permission of the translators.

"Pine Garden," "Fragment," and "Grain Buds" by Yang Mu. From *Hawk of the Mind: Collected Poems*. NY: Columbia University Press, 2018. Reprinted by permission of the translators.

"Crossing Half of China to Sleep with You" and "On the Threshing Floor, I Chase Chickens Away" by Yu Xiuhua, translated by Ming Di. From *World Literature Today* 92:4 (July/August 2018). Reprinted by permission of the translator.

"Association of Absolute Aesthetics" and "The Books of the Original Role" by Zang Di. From *New Cathay: Contemporary Chinese Poetry*, edited by Ming Di. North Adams, MA: Tupelo Press, 2013; also from *The Book of Cranes: Poems by Zang Di*, translated by Ming Di and Neil Aitken. Australia: Vagabond Press, 2015.